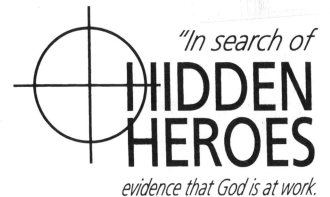

"In search of HIDDEN HEROES

evidence that God is at work.

Don Moore
Lorna Dueck

FT
PUBLICATIONS

Faith Today Publications is the publishing division of the Evangelical Fellowship of Canada.

Scripture quotations marked (TM) are from THE MESSAGE. Copyright © 1993. Used by permission of NavPress Publishing Group.

Scripture quotations from Psalms marked (TM) are from THE MESSAGE PSALMS. Copyright © 1994. Used by permission of NavPress Publishing Group.

Other Scripture quotations are taken from the HOLY BIBLE, NEW INTERNATIONAL VERSION. Copyright © 1973, 1978, 1984 International Bible Society.

Printed and bound in Canada by Hignell printing Limited

Canadian Cataloguing in Publication Data

Main entry under title:

In search of hidden heroes : evidence that God is at work

Includes bibliographical references.
ISBN 0-9695596-4-X

1. Evangelistic work – Canada. 2. Evangeliaries – Canada – Biography. I. Moore, Donald J. (Donald John), 1953-   . II. Dueck, Lorna, 1959-   .

BV3780.I5 1995   269'.2'092271   C95-930025-2

Faith Today Publications
#1, 175 Riviera Drive
Markham, Ontario   L3R 5J6
Canada

CONTENTS

FOREWORD

Every day our headlines tell us of a world in crisis. Wars rage, crime skyrockets, families disintegrate – the fabric of society itself appears to be coming apart at the seams. But do the headlines tell the whole story?

No, they do not – as this book vividly illustrates. Amid the apparent chaos and conflicts of our world God is still at work through the lives of individual men and women who are committed to Christ and are seeking to serve Him. These stories do not often make the daily news; yet from the standpoint of eternity they are the real headlines – the events that will have eternal significance.

In Search of Hidden Heroes will encourage all who read it, demonstrating that God still delights in using ordinary people to do extraordinary things. Its chronicle of "hidden heroes" who are involved in evangelism in dozens of ways throughout Canada deserves to be told, and will be a challenge to all believers to be witnesses for Christ wherever God has placed them.

May this book inspire countless Christians – not just in Canada but elsewhere – to a deeper commitment and a renewed vision to become "hidden heroes" for Christ, going forth in God's strength to bring the light of the gospel to those around them.

Billy Graham

PREFACE

"Don't shuffle along, eyes to the ground, absorbed with the things right in front of you. Look up and be alert to what is going on around Christ – that's where the action is. See things from his perspective." (Colossians 3:2,3 TM)

How you understand and enjoy life is a matter of what you see or do not see. It is all a matter of perspective. Taking a closer look at the people that God is using opens our eyes to vast possibilities. From God's perspective, there are countless individuals who in their own unique ways are making significant contributions to His kingdom. In many ways, they are really "Hidden Heroes."

Heroes are the faith-infusers of our lives, fresh examples that God still works miracles in individuals today. We nurture our faith through fellowship and reading Scripture, but sometimes the best incentive is the personal example that shows that God's hero could be you or me.

Heroes are not only people who perform great deeds in extraordinary situations, but are often born out of everyday lives, and often not really discovered until they are gone. This book brings to your attention some unknown people in the fabric of Canadian life: people running difficult races, reaching unreached peoples, carrying their faith outside of their churches and into their communities. These are ordinary people who in their own quiet ways deserve to be counted the contemporary equivalent of Hebrews chapter 11.

May this book serve to inspire countless more hidden heroes to arise from these stories of people who are reaching out to their world with the gospel.

Brian C. Stiller

INTRODUCTION

"Hidden Hero":
a low-profile person with a high impact for the kingdom

Is there evidence that God is at work in our nation? Wanting to know, I set out on a search from coast to coast to find that evidence. Simply put, who is engaging in evangelism? How are they doing it?

As I began to search, and then to tell others the stories I heard, I discovered that people were filled with a fresh sense of hope. It became clear that what God's people need the most is: *hope!* And the hope is based on the evidence that God is at work. Soon I discovered scores of God's people peppered across our land who, in their own unique ways, are being used significantly by God to influence the people of Canada.

I found myself pondering how the stories of these special people could be told. As I and others explored the creative possibilities, the idea emerged of initiating a nationwide hunt entitled "In Search of Hidden Heroes – Evidence that God is at Work."

With much prayer and a clear sense of God's leading, we began the intense search. Catching the vision, dozens of denominations and parachurch ministries across the nation joined in helping to distribute the "search materials." Within weeks the excitement grew as we began to receive what ultimately would be hundreds of "Hidden Heroes" to be followed up. With fascination, we watched as the contacts began to reflect a colourful array. In story after story, I could feel the beating hearts of a wide cross-section of committed Canadians representing all ages, regions and many professions and ethnic communities.

As the stories unfolded, I wrestled with the best way to describe these ordinary people who had been identified as "Hidden Heroes." I came to the realization that a "Hidden Hero" is really *a low-profile person with a high impact for the kingdom.* The psalmist, said it well: *"Break open your words, let the light shine out, let ordinary people see the meaning."* Psalm 119:130 (TM)

Coauthor Lorna Dueck recruited more than a dozen freelance researchers and writers to join our efforts in producing a resource of more than 100 stories from which to select. Then, laying the stories out on the table before the Lord, I began to pray for wisdom and insight to identify the common threads that could weave these stories into the fabric of a book that would inspire God's people with hope. You now hold the result in your hands.

Without exception, every "Hidden Hero" in this book has said in one form or another that, although his or her story is being told, each has a strong sense that it is really God who deserves the recognition and glory. By His grace, every Christian in Canada has the same potential for God to use him or her as one of His "Hidden Heroes" to reach our nation with His love. May the stories of these "Hidden Heroes" provide occasion for you and I to *celebrate God and the gospel at work.*

Don Moore
January 1995

— VISION 2000 CANADA IS A MINISTRY OF THE EVANGELICAL FELLOWSHIP OF CANADA —

ACKNOWLEDGEMENTS

This book is the result of hundreds of Canadians picking up pen or phone to suggest the name of a "hero." For all of you who helped in that process, either by submitting names or publicizing our search, thank you for giving us the scoop. God ultimately deserves the glory for what He has done through these lives.

Hidden Heroes: We thank the many heroes who shared openly and vulnerably with us in the interview process, opening your life experience to us, trusting it would be used to encourage the Christian church into action. Your lives have challenged, enriched and blessed all of us who were involved in the search. A special bouquet each who wrote your own testimony and worked with us as we adapted your sharing into these pages.

National steering committee: We express our appreciation to the Vision 2000 Canada National Steering Committee for their commitment to this specific project and the special working team of Bruce Stacey, Bill McRae, Geoff Tunnicliffe and David Collins, where the idea of Hidden Heroes emerged.

Researchers and writers: We acknowledge the following researchers and writers who made contributions to this project: Alan Doerksen, Debra Fieguth, Bill Fledderus, Lori Gwynne, Russ Hiebert, William Kennedy, Nan McKenzie Kosowan, Anna-Liza Kozma, Chrystie Kroeker, Nancy Lindquist, Joel Lundy, Linda McGibbon, Eric Nelson, Lori Regehr, Karen Segal, Marjie Smith, Sandra Smith and Kim Steele.

Editorial advisory committee: A special thank-you goes to *ChristianWeek* publisher Harold Jantz, who chaired our advisory committee and to the committee: Paul Wartman, Murray Henderson, Deanna Waters and Ernesto Pinto.

Manuscript editors: Special acknowledgements to the editors who painstakingly went through the entire manuscript giving us insightful advice and direction for the finished book you now hold in your hand: Denise O'Leary, Tim Pigeau, Mark Rodgers, Eric Stolte and Mark Weller.

Design and production: Thanks to Krista Marshall and Marla Schultz for the hours of data entry, Leighton Wiebe (NEXT Communications Inc) for the graphic design of the book.

Leaders and ministries: Thanks to Brian C. Stiller (Evangelical Fellowship of Canada) and David Mainse (Crossroads Family of Ministries) for their enthusiasm and support throughout this entire project. Thanks also to the many denominations and parachurch ministries for distributing the Hidden Hero search materials to their respective churches and ministries.

Our families: We thank our spouses, Werner Dueck and Darla Moore, who each put up with a flurry of faxes, phone calls, voice mail and our occasional creative bursts of emotion. And thanks to our children, Adam and Elise Dueck and David and Dianne Moore, for their excitement and joy of life that kept us "sane."

Don Moore, Lorna Dueck

WON BY ONE

What does it take for a person to make a significant decision or change in life? What appears to be a simple "yes/no" decision is often the outcome of a process involving many influential people, events and circumstances. For example, consider the case of Frank.

Returning home from work tired, Frank plopped into the sofa armed with his clicker. As the channels flipped by on command, he was suddenly captivated by a slick, smooth commercial for Chrysler's new "Intrepid." With his aging car rusting away in the garage, he would have to keep this new model in mind.

Early the next morning, on the way to his garage he noticed that his neighbour had a new Intrepid parked in the driveway. Frank stopped to comment. His neighbour waxed eloquent about the merits of his new purchase. Arriving at work, Frank found his mail opened on his desk, awaiting his attention. With a little time before his first meeting, he sat back, coffee in hand, and glanced through the new issue of *Maclean's* magazine. One of the first advertisements that caught his eye described – guess what? – features of the new Chrysler Intrepid. He read it with interest, then set it aside to pursue the day ahead.

Back in his old car, Frank found himself stuck in rush hour traffic. He turned on the radio to hear a favourite sports feature only to discover it was sponsored by Chrysler of Canada who announced, of course, the new Intrepid. Then his eyes caught a flashy billboard displaying the new Intrepid life-sized in all its glory. Almost without thinking, he decided to swing by the local Chrysler dealership to test drive one. And it turned out there was a salesman available, more than ready to show it to him. Frank was soon the proud owner of a brand new Intrepid.

What caused Frank to decide to buy that new car? Was it the TV ad, the neighbour, the magazine ad, the radio ad, the billboard or the salesman? The answer is really "all of the above." Significant decisions are usually informed by many sources that help to shape our knowledge and attitudes, leading us to take specific action.

The same process is at work when it comes to spiritual decision making. In fact, studies done with individuals who made a commitment to Christ in the '80s show that the average person had seven contacts with the gospel message before making a commitment. Because this continues to be the case in the '90s, Christians need to affirm a multiplicity of approaches and presentations of the gospel to those who have yet to respond. Although it may take only one person to assist in making the ultimate decision, there are countless others involved in the process. Each of us has a role to play in influencing people around us to consider a relationship with Christ. You and I may not know whether our connection with that undecided person is the first, third or seventh contact with the gospel.

4 ——

We each have the responsibility to represent the person of Jesus to others. Each of us has different abilities and gifts from God that He will use if we simply make them available. As in the stories that follow, whether in a coffee shop, airplane or high school, God wants to use our availability to let His Spirit guide our conversations and involvements to express His love to a hurting world.

— dm

Pray diligently. Stay alert, with your eyes wide open in gratitude. Don't forget to pray for us, that God will open doors for telling the mystery of Christ. . . . Pray that every time I open my mouth I'll be able to make Christ plain as day to them. Use your heads as you live and work among outsiders. . . . Make the most of every opportunity. Be gracious in your speech. The goal is to bring the best out in others in a conversation, not to put them down, not to cut them out.

Colossians 4 (TM)

HIS LEGACY:
A COFFEE MUG

The white coffee mug was a common enough sight to anyone who
drops in to Tim Horton doughnut shops. What was unfamiliar was the
location. It sat on a casket. That mug was a fitting symbol for the
life and ministry of Tom White.

From bush pilot to waterbed salesman, union arbitrator to music distributor, Tom White was a born entrepreneur. A regular around London, Ontario coffee shops, he was the kind of fellow who never seemed to work but always had plenty of money. He was well known to the police, and was at one time a ruthless businessman. Tom had been described as an "insensitive, belligerent, foul-mouthed atheist." Then, over a period of a few months ten years ago, things began to change.

Tom became attracted to a woman who attended a local church. As their friendship developed over the months, he was drawn into other relationships with people in the church. Occasionally he and pastor Don Howard would go out for lunch. At one of those meetings the pastor gave Tom some prophecy tapes. Immediately Tom was hooked. He began reading everything he could on prophecy and the end times. A short time later he trusted God and became a new creature in Christ.

Soon the new Tom White began to be known around town. Now when the middle-aged, heavyset man entered a coffee shop, some patrons headed for the nearest exit. But most gave him a friendly greeting as he got his coffee and walked over to join the conversation. Eventually, the talk would shift to current affairs, and Tom would lean forward and interject, "But that shouldn't surprise you. It's all been predicted."

This was to be a common pattern of his life for the next several years. Rising early, Tom made the rounds to the coffee shops before lunch. Sometimes he had appointments to keep. Then he returned home to sleep for several hours. After dinner he began his visits again until the small hours of the morning. He found that the coffee shops were an ideal place to meet people in need. Over the years, he met hundreds of people and developed many friends.

Among these were some of the city's pastors. If Tom met a needy individual he thought could best be helped by a pastor, he would make arrangements for the two to meet. Or he might send a person to one of the neighbourhood churches. The back pew of Tom's own church was often filled with people he had directed there. Over time people were helped, befriended and sometimes saved.

Often it was in the midst of personal turmoil that Tom was most used by the Lord. The woman who had first drawn him to the church gradually lost interest in him and eventually married someone else. But having experienced rejection, Tom was able to comfort and encourage people whose marriages were falling apart. To those struggling in business or with other problems, Tom gave a listening ear. He sent flowers. He dropped in for a chat. He was "an encourager, big time," as one friend put it.

Eugene Gendron experienced Tom's ministry to his own family. He initially met Tom at his daughter's doughnut shop. Soon the two of them were having long discussions about God. Tom spent many hours at Eugene's home and gradually became like a member of the family. They all began attending Tom's church and Eugene's daughter rededicated her life to the Lord. Six months later Eugene himself trusted the Lord for salvation.

That was an event that Tom was not to witness, however. In the fall of 1992, he was diagnosed with inoperable throat cancer. He faced the news head on. He made arrangements for his funeral and bought a burial plot. Then he returned to the coffee shops.

One evening in November 1993, Tom telephoned a friend and asked for a ride to a nearby doughnut shop. Having developed a tremor in his left leg, he was unable to drive himself. The two visited with several others for a few hours. Then Tom began to tire and his friend drove him home. Early the next morning Tom died.

At his funeral were many people who had been touched by Tom's ministry over the years and others he led to the Lord. A number of street people, Tim Horton employees, and old and new friends stood up to give a word of testimony about him. When one of them was asked what he best remembered Tom White for, he replied, "for the circle of friends that he introduced me to."

It was not Tom's ability that made him special. It was his availability.

T O O   S O O N   O L D ,
T O O   L A T E   S M A R T

For six years, Bligh Stockwell presented himself on the doorsteps of a large housing complex in Vancouver. It left him with the unshakable conviction that focused, personal contact is the best way to reach our country for Christ. It is just one aspect of wisdom he has gleaned from nearly fifty years of searching God and our culture for keys to open hearts of the unsaved. There are literally hundreds of Canadians who can trace their conversion to the work of Bligh and his wife Audrey.

Trained as a chemist, I was standing at my workbench, looking out over Great Slave Lake one day when I received a very clear call of God on my life. It was a message in my heart and mind that I knew was from God. He gave me a vision of a life in Christian service that was to be integrated with my secular employment. I was to be a self-supporting worker in God's kingdom.

A year later I moved to Ottawa and met Audrey, my future wife and co-worker. Immediately we commenced a church replanting project in a village where the only evidence of a once thriving church was a vacant building. Soon, with the help of other young people, the old hall was cleaned and filled with young people, new believers and few of the old saints who returned to rejoice with us.

The fire of new life spread quickly to another village where I was invited to lead an outreach Bible study. This study group became a spiritual life growth cell and developed into a thriving church within about three years.

During this time (1950-56) I commuted to Ottawa to earn a living as a metallurgical chemist, and spent evenings and week-ends doing church planting work in the villages.

By 1956 we again felt the call of God and through my work as a metallurgist we moved to Coquitlam, B.C. The church planting vision was very much alive in our hearts but were not sure how we would do that. Early in our move, however, a dedicated Christian woman in the public school system arrived at our door and asked if we would help with a high school Bible club.

We gave it a try, and the very first night Audrey had opportunity to lead a young boy, Barry, to Christ. (He is now a head elder in his church and has been a constant encouragement to us over the years.) Barry, Charly, a young French immigrant and an ex-missionary couple became foundation stones in a new church we began to plant later that year. Austin Avenue Chapel began in a rented corner store, and eventually grew to about 280.

But, and this is an important BUT, there was something about our church planting experience in both Ontario and British Columbia that I found disturbing. We had not significantly penetrated the alien pagan culture around us. We had planted churches, but not within the majority secular society, the real mission field. Most of the growth had come through Christians on the move or second generation Christian rebels returning to their roots.

Disappointed by that reality, in 1980 we did a preliminary survey of 240 families in a low-cost subsidized housing area. This provided a wake-up jolt to our evangelical mindset when we learned that at least ninety-five percent of these people would never be receptive to conventional church and parachurch approaches.

So for two years we paid door-to-door visits to every residence each week. We asked parents if they would send their children to a Sunday school we held in the complex's day-care. If a new child came to our club, we would visit her parents and explain that "Sandra appeared at our club and we just want you to know what we're all about." We called this approach "through-the-child" evangelism.

The result was that a Bible study soon started in a woman's basement and we began seeing people grow into new life in Christ. It took months, and in some cases years, for people to talk through their hurts, their misperceptions of church and religion. As that Bible study grew, we continued, for the next four years, to visit every residence once a month.

People began to open up to us as they realized that we did not fit their stereotypes of church and religion. That started removal of half the wall against evangelism, the other half of the wall was our own misperceptions of secular society.

As we acclimatized to their culture, reality dawned that change had to happen first in us; we must become loving, appreciative and open towards the people we hoped to reach, accepting of the morally neutral elements of their pagan culture.

Now, in the senior phase of life, we can identify with Corrie ten Boom, who said, "too soon old, too late smart." But we believe that others will carry the torch of focused evangelism through the wall of misperception and into the hearts of secular Canada.

We pray for younger families who will ask for a leave from their churches and put all those church time energies into reaching their neighbourhoods, families who would work as national missionaries, doing cross-cultural missions right here in Canada. If a church could release a couple to do this in their own neighbourhood, you would see a home fellowship group of about six families within a year. Within three years, I believe there is a definite possibility of that group growing to at least fifty. Understandably, it will take three to four years of incubation in the home church groups before these new believers can be integrated into an existing church because our evangelical culture is so different from theirs.

In my home province of British Columbia, fewer than four percent of the population attend any place of worship. Oh how we need real missionaries to Canada.

10 ——

■

R E - E N T R Y   F R O M   E X I L E

*As vice-president of the Buddhist association of British Columbia,
Tin Kyi was nagged by a conflict that kept resurfacing in his life.
Why was his belief in Lord Buddha being challenged by the lives
of those who believed in Lord Jesus? Here he describes the
heroes who helped him discover the answer.*

I was born in 1930, the eldest son of an affluent Buddhist family in Burma. Because of my father's early death in an air crash, my family gave me nearly unconditional respect as the eldest son. This respect motivated me to avoid evil, as I was now the father figure.

I studied science and mathematics, graduating from university as a statistician. Through good fortune I was employed by an American consulting firm working in Burma. Later I moved to the Department of Trade, a crown corporation where I advanced to the highest civil service posting at thirty-six years of age. My life, as you can see, was "on track." But suddenly things changed.

Due to a change of government, I was "offered" retirement. This offer meant I would be unable to work in my country, nor could I invest my small savings. In other words, my retirement would lead me into poverty or force my departure. This environment led me to immigrate to Canada in 1969. Shortly after, my wife Joyce and our two children followed me.

— 11

I was alone when I first arrived in Victoria but a Canadian took me in. Based on a recommendation from a mutual friend, this man assisted in my immigration and landed status process. Even more, he provided a fully furnished home and a warmth of welcome that I could hardly believe. I look back now and realize that his motivation was his Christian faith.

This act of kindness reminded me that from my earliest memories Christians had been a significant part of my life. I had attended both Roman Catholic and Baptist grade schools. Furthermore, my mother, although a Buddhist all her life, often socialized within the Christian community.

Then there was my wife Joyce, who helped me on my path to Jesus. She was born into a Christian home and believed early in her life. Her life has been that of a Christian wife and mother to my children, and also a professional in her career. Her way was never forceful. Instead she would say to me, "Tin, I am weak. If I did not have faith in Christ, I do not know what I would do. I wish you had faith, even in something."

Finally, it was a confrontation with a serious illness that brought to me what my Buddhism could not provide: someone to whom I could turn.

Buddhism is really a great philosophy but there is no God to trust; there is no one "out there." In the spring of 1993 I was diagnosed with advanced cancer of the bowel. This caused me to turn again to the debate that had been ongoing for years, the debate between Lord Buddha and Lord Jesus.

The third "hero" then came to my mind. In 1970 I came into contact with Bernard Khaw, a Burmese of Chinese heritage who was attending university. He was exceptionally brilliant and a faithful, sure Christian. We had an uncle-nephew relationship and we would have discussions regarding Christianity. Now, as I was dealing with advanced cancer, some words from Bernard came back to me twenty years after he spoke them.

"Uncle Tin," he said, "if you argue and do not have faith, you cannot become a Christian."

At this point, as I faced death, I asked my wife if I could see her pastor, Cal Netterfield. He was a family friend and pastored the Vancouver church where my wife and children were members. With my family present, I asked him if he could help me become a Christian. In the hospital that night before surgery I confessed my sins to Jesus Christ and asked Him to accept me. The arguments continue, but no longer about who is Lord. I know that Jesus is Lord.

By the way, surgery (actually three) was successful. I am well and I give thanks to Jesus Christ for His healing. As a gift to me one night while I drifted in and out of consciousness He gave me a vision of angels ministering to me. This was a great comfort during those dark hours.

The fourth "hero" is my daughter Moe. She read to me, prayed with me and was my teacher during those long days of recovery. She is our strong-minded child and I suppose most happy that I am a believer in Jesus Christ.

My baptism on Father's Day 1994 was a significant event in which I was able to share with many of my Buddhist friends about my new faith.

As I ponder the reasons for my "final surrender," I believe there are two: I trust Christ because I know now He is the creator, but even more important, that this Creator has forgiven me.

■

A WORD IN EDGEWISE

Waste disposal consultant Len Remple was chairing a session with 200 business delegates when the chief presenter walked in half an hour late for the meeting. When the tardy but distinguished expert rumbled "Oh, for Christ's sake" into his open microphone, Len replied to the crowd, "Oh, that's wonderful; I do everything for Christ's sake also." That kind of boldness has given Len dozens of opportunities to bring individuals to the saving knowledge of Jesus Christ. Here he shares one such encounter.

Flying out of Vancouver one Monday morning my mind was whirling with the pressure of making final preparations for the budget meeting I was to attend in Toronto. I needed solitude and was happy the seat next to me was empty. During takeoff, a flight attendant named Sandy sat down beside me and soon asked whether or not I enjoyed my frequent trips.

"Yes and no," I replied. "I enjoy the business but I don't like being away from my family." She asked about my family and I asked about hers.

"I'm thirty-two, never married and I've got the greatest Mom, Dad, and seven siblings. We're a family that likes to get together often and enjoy one another," she said.

"So do we," I replied. "And in our family we have a special bond that binds us together."

"What do you mean by 'a special bond?'" was her offhand, half-interested remark.

"I'll tell you about that but first I want your permission to explain it in full, so that you'll understand what I mean."

14 ——— "Go ahead. It can't be all that difficult to grasp."

"Well, I have a personal relationship with Jesus Christ and so do my family members," I stated. Then I explained that God, our Father, has a way for us to become members of His family, through adoption.

"It's as simple as ABC," I said. "A – admit I'm a sinner. B – believe that Jesus Christ is God's only way to Himself. C – Confess that I accept Jesus Christ to rule my life."

Her response was friendly but indifferent.

"My life is perfectly in order, relationally, financially, morally and physically. I don't need God in my life." With that Sandy excused herself to serve the meal.

I began to pray. "Lord, she has no apparent need. Reveal to me how to penetrate that self-sufficiency and cause her to see her need of You."

When she sat down again I asked her why, as a mature, independent woman, she keeps returning home to visit her dad. "Why not stay away, enjoy the pleasures of life and ignore Dad?" I probed.

Her reply was swift.

"Dad says the family is incomplete unless we are in harmony and together. He lives just to see us, hug us and talk with us. Even if I could stay away, I wouldn't because it would tear Dad apart." She choked at my callous suggestion.

Gently I replied, "That's how our heavenly Father feels when you ignore Him. He loves you dearly and says, 'I stand at the door and knock. If you will open your life to me, I'll come in and dine with you.' God says, 'Sandy, my family is incomplete without you. Won't you come home? My heart breaks for you to come home.' "

She looked at me, said nothing and left to attend to pre-landing duties. While I was leaving the terminal with my baggage I saw her running toward me. She grabbed my elbow and, tears pouring freely, she sobbed six words: "You got me. You got me!"

At that she turned and ran, and I have never seen her since. I pray the Holy Spirit will take over.

With many persons I meet, I can find a bridge in the conversation that conveniently allows me to say I am a follower of Jesus Christ. In this situation, family was the instant bridge.

Although the depth of conversation varies, I find that encounters like the one with Sandy happen to me several dozen times a year. I can honestly say that in the past fifteen years I have not found one single person who was offended by my approach.

I have often thought, if every Christian would go to hell for one day and return to earth, everyone would suddenly have the "gift of evangelism."

■

No Middle Ground

In every Christian organization, you will find a behind-the-scenes champion, someone who carries the ball, cheers the tired, stabilizes the crises and becomes an invaluable part of what God is doing. At Vision 2000 Canada, Tim Pigeau is just that kind of person.

"So what reasons do you have this week for not becoming a Christian?" Joe's question irritated me.

"The audacity of him to be so personal and tell me how I should live," I thought. But Joe was my roommate and in the previous few months he had shown me a love and acceptance I had not encountered in my life.

I never knew my father, and my mother was killed in a car accident when I was six. I temporarily lived with my grandparents until my grandmother had a stroke during breakfast and my grandfather died of cancer a few years later. I was adopted by a friend of the family but things continued to worsen emotionally during my teen years. Miscommunication, misunderstanding, and emotional abuse were my companions growing up.

Excelling in studies gave me a measure of significance through high school, but my University of British Columbia days taught me more than just science. My roommate Joe Harrison, a senior who curiously elected for a shared room in the student residence, had many engaging late-night (early morning) discussions with me about philosophy of life, God and science which began to erode my impressions of the Christian life as dull and belief in God as irrational.

Many of Joe's Christian friends would come by to visit him, often striking up conversation with me. Although I'd had good friends in high school, I experienced love and acceptance from these guys as I never had before. Meanwhile, Joe began asking me to help him review the Scripture verses he was memorizing. More out of generosity than curiosity, I quizzed Joe almost daily and as weeks passed, I saw more than eighty Bible verses and had "inadvertently" memorized many of them. I had no idea that Joe and his friends were praying for me to come to Christ. They were asking God to shake my confidence in my academic and organizational abilities because they sensed that my achievements were barriers to trusting Christ. In hindsight, it was no wonder I failed my first exam and kept losing my wallet and keys. Years later, I also learned that my Mom's best friend Connie had been praying for me for years.

By the start of second semester Joe was regularly asking, "So what reasons do you have this week for not becoming a Christian?" Much as I disliked the question, the urging was helpful as each week brought new reasons that led to a fresh discussion. "No Middle Ground" was the title of the Scripture memory verse one week: Matthew 12:30, "He who is not with me is against me, and he who does not gather with me scatters." Because I wasn't opposed to Jesus, some days the decision hung over me. I struggled through each barrier – intellectual, emotional and ultimately spiritual – to accepting Christ as my saviour: the veracity of the Bible, the existence of God, possible rejection by others, and selfishness.

Walking home from class one day, I admired the foliage and breathed the fresh sea breeze and was suddenly swept by the idea of God as a creator (unlike what the biochemistry textbook taught). I became aware of the chasm of sin that separated me from God. In fact, the more I thought about how Jesus lived, I was beginning to see just how different I was from God and how I needed Him in my life. Eyes open, stepping through the residence doors, my first meaningful prayer naturally followed: "God if you are real, I give my life over to you."

When I told Joe, he excitedly quizzed me with questions like, "How do you know God heard you?" and "How do you know you have eternal life?" to each of which I recited the memory verses "Assurance of Answered Prayer" (John 16:24) and "Assurance of Salvation" (1 John 5:11,12).

My Christian acquaintances became for me like a family I never knew. A tremendously supportive group of friends began anchoring me in my spiritual walk.

I was fully prepared to rub shoulders with one of Canada's unreached sectors – researchers – but the Lord has clearly directed me, as suited by the abilities He has given me, into occupational ministry. But I still carry the vision of roommate ministry. Since my own experience on the receiving end I have ministered to students in residence at the University of Saskatchewan and now live in a shared townhouse. As a single person, I have the opportunity at this stage of my life to be involved personally in the lives of roommates who are not yet Christians.

■

SUCCESS OUT OF CONTROL

Susan S. was applauded when she told an audience of 6,500 recovering alcoholics that Jesus was her higher power to a life free from addiction. Alcoholics Anonymous is a family she has been a part of for the past five years. She believes God led her to AA because her lifestyle was an embarrassment to Him. Within AA's twelve steps to health she found the key to sharing her faith in Christ.

I grew up in a religious family that was neglectful and dysfunctional. In my teen years, I sensed I wasn't worth being with but I discovered that alcohol made me feel changed. I became sexually promiscuous, had borne three children by the time I was nineteen, and crashed a marriage by the time I was twenty-one.

But I was good at building a career. By the time I was thirty, I was travelling the country in charge of sixty retail stores. It was pretty heady stuff. I had relied heavily on alcohol and sleeping around but I was getting to the point that I couldn't keep up with that game anymore. The alcohol wasn't working like it used to, my mind was racing, and I was a hyper mess.

Right around that time I began to be aware that God was there. Some childhood prayers began coming back to me. One day, riding home, the Lord's prayer came into my head. THY WILL BE DONE was impressed upon me as though it was printed in capital letters in my brain. That night, I had a profound spiritual experience with God and had a real sense that He was being a daddy to me, a father right there to hold me.

I talked about this spiritual experience at work and discovered that a friend there was a Christian. She gave me a Bible and I fell in love with reading it. But it seemed the only way I could stay away from drinking was to not go anywhere. As a result, I withdrew from everything and read my Bible and, frankly, grew very flaky.

I was also in a financial mess – the gap between my income and my bills was $300 a week. By now I had gathered that God could handle money a lot better than I could and I believed that if I would tithe, God would fix my money dilemma.

I didn't attend church but I began dropping off $100 a week at little church plant that had started in the school down the street. Those people became so committed to love me that I started going to their church. About twenty percent of this small group were Bible college theologians and they helped me see I was worshipping in the spirit but not in truth. They were not at all emotional and would not tolerate someone as flaky as I, but what they did do was teach me truth with a capital T and love me.

The pastor there would often preach his sermons in a Johnny Carson style. He would set up the stage like a talk-show set and interview people. One morning he interviewed a recovered alcoholic. Well, the guy was telling my story and it was exactly what I needed. Although I had been a Christian for eight years now, I still didn't have victory over alcohol. I talked to this man after the sermon and he gave me a little AA book and took me to Alcoholics Anonymous.

AA's principles line up completely with the Bible and they really work. One of the first steps is to meaningfully take complete stock of who you are and where you are at. That is a big step to getting right with Christ if you allow it to be. The combination of my new church home and the twelve steps is what made it for me.

The final step in AA is to take what you have so freely been given and give it to others. That really excited me. I had news that was so good, how could I not share it? AA is a wonderful place to share the gospel. I usually go weekly, and I find there are always people who ask what I have that works so well for recovery.

I usually say something like, "Well, I don't know if you're ready for this but it's not just the twelve steps that healed me; it's Jesus." I explain about salvation. Sometimes they back up at 100 mph but other times they listen. I share my own experience and if they are interested, I invite them to church or a Bible study. I took one friend to McDonald's to meet my pastor and she prayed to become a Christian right there.

The little church plant that showed me Christ has since closed and now I attend two churches, one in the morning for its strong teaching, a different one in the evening for its warm, enthusiastic environment. I have to say, though, that even though I am deeply committed to the church, AA does a way better job of loving people than most churches do.

I have brought tons of people to church but I've had to slow that down because Christians are just so awkward about accepting these people. I caution church goers to pray that they won't flinch when people with a rough background come into their circles. Recently a friend started going to church and became a Christian, so I introduced her to a cell group for discipleship. She has back-combed hair, wears short skirts and has a pretty tumultuous past.

"Susan, you should have seen their faces when I started sharing," she told me. "They're not ready for me yet." So she has stopped going to church.

Alcoholics really need Jesus. Please pray to love these people. Just love them. That is what will attract them to Christ.

■

—— 21

T H E S T R E E T — M Y H O M E

In Calgary there is a dynamic street ministry that cares for 350 people a day, and ushers many into Christian faith. The Mustard Seed's executive director Pat Nixon is a former street person himself. Pat was nominated more than once as a hidden hero, and he is renowned in Canada for his love and insight into healing broken lives. As Pat tells his story, he explains that the real hidden heroes are the lay people of Calgary who loved him into Christian service.

What's different about today? I crawl out from under a soiled mattress in an abandoned shed that I've claimed as home. I didn't sleep much as the nights are cold and my poor health has left me shivering a lot. There are no more tears; I shed them all long ago in the quiet of the night, where no one hears me and no one really cares. I'm a street kid and have been that way since I was twelve. For the past three years I've existed with petty crime, drugs and booze. I smell from months without washing. I'm a con who plays on the pity of the affluent for the sake of gaining change to buy a bottle of Lysol or a tube of glue.

Today will be like yesterday which was much like the day before. As I walk through the crowds, people will make a path for me. They will turn their eyes, adjust their course and pretend they have not seen me. But they do see me and I hope to corner them in order to obtain their tokens of pity.

But today's panhandle turned up something entirely different. They were a peculiar people, of which three, Rod, Rob and Carl would become the most clear examples of compassion that I have ever experienced. As they met me head on, I tried to panhandle a few bucks from them. They were not ignorant of my intentions yet they did not humiliate me be revealing their knowledge of my ways. Their response was without hesitation.

"We have no money to give you but we will buy you something to eat."

I willingly followed them to a restaurant, interested in their strange behaviour but equally concerned about their intentions. I attacked the food that was placed before me, wolfing it down like a dog, afraid that someone would snatch it away before I had finished. I searched the faces at the table only to discover their heads bowed in prayer. I did not pray with them as I knew nothing of the God they honoured. All I could expect of people like them was a tract filled with pictures and words I would not understand. Then they would go away.

How I had misjudged them. I was soon to discover that their

intentions were not governed by their own desires but by God's desires. That is not to say they were robots completing a programed task with no conscience or choice, for they chose to be with me, evident by the compassion that so easily flowed through their words and actions.

"Why don't you come with us to our coffee house? It's called the Burning Bush." Why not go with them? I had nothing to lose and soon they would discover they had nothing to gain. The coffee house was in the basement of a church and was filled with people like Rod, Rob and Carl, all of whom went out of their way to see to my comfort. They purchased pop for me and sat with me as I listened to the music. They didn't make me feel silly when I asked inappropriate questions or made distasteful remarks like, "Hey, do you guys party often?" or "That girl on the stage sure looks great."

— 23

As the evening moved on my new friends asked, "Do you believe in Jesus Christ?" I told them that my father claimed that Jesus was a sorcerer and the only time I had been given a Bible was from some people who came to our door when I was a young boy.

These friends then gently explained who Jesus was and that He died to forgive my sin and to give me eternal life. That night I prayed openly that Jesus would come into my life. Although Rod, Rob and Carl celebrated my verbal commitment, in all honesty, who I truly accepted was them. Their friendship and love were so evident that I would have been devastated to go back to my shed thinking that I would not see them again.

But that night Rod and Rob took me into their home. They clothed me, fed me, encouraged me to deal with my addictions, forgave me when I stole from them and lied to them, visited me in prison when I made more serious mistakes, and challenged me to be more than I thought I could be. It was through their consistent

and laboured acts of love that I finally saw clearly the awesome
love of Jesus and believed Him to be true. Many would see these
men like any others who passed through a church door, but don't
let their appearance deceive you – these men exemplify Christ.
Their love for me, as demonstrated by their consistency and self
sacrifice, changed my life.

Today, and all future days, will never be the same again.

SIGNIFICANT
RELATIONSHIPS

During lunch with Michael McAteer, religion editor at *The Toronto Star*, Lorna Dueck almost choked on her fork when he said, "The problem with you Christians is you're always trying to convert everyone. In our pluralistic society that isn't acceptable. Just love people for a change. That's the way it's supposed to be and if they want to know more about your Christianity, fine."

All of us long to be loved for who we are. When mutual respect and trust are nurtured, opportunities emerge to listen and learn about what is really important to each other. In our exuberance to share the gospel, we sometimes forget that one key way God communicates Himself to us is through relationships. The essence of the gospel is a relationship with God's son, Jesus Christ. By initiating relationships with others they begin to sense the need for change because they experience God's character reflected through His son in us. —— 27

Within caring relationships, people are drawn into a love that is unusual and worth exploring. People who first discover how much you care might then want to listen to what you have to share. An overly zealous individual can unintentionally give the wrong impression, however. No one wants to be a "pet project," used to accomplish another person's goals, even if the goals are good.

I am fascinated with Jesus' relationships in the Gospels. Some were clearly intentional, and others rose out of the normal course of everyday events. His relationships included both the least respected and the most respected people in society. Each relationship reflected His ability to demonstrate God's love and to "strike the responsive chord" of a need in another's life. In the following stories, you will discover that through relationships these "Hidden Heroes" have a high impact for the kingdom's sake. It is worth remembering that the closer my relationship is to God, the more alert I will be to the significant relationships He wants me to nurture for the kingdom.

– dm

Even though I am free of the demands and expectations of everyone, I have voluntarily become a servant to any and all in order to reach a wide range of people: religious, nonreligious, meticulous moralists, loose-living immoralists, the defeated, the demoralized – whoever. I didn't take on their way of life. I kept my bearings in Christ – but I entered their world and tried to experience things from their point of view. I've become just about every sort of servant there is in my attempts to lead those I meet into a God-saved life.

I Corinthians 9 (TM)

THE CANADIAN CONNECTION

Helping newcomers to Canada feel welcome is an art Barb Lehto practises on and off her job. But as a Christian employed by the government in Immigration Services, can she bring the gospel of Jesus as part of her working policy in refugee settlement?

"My most important role at work is as a person of integrity dealing with people," explains Barb. She spends long hours helping people who come to Canada seeking a better life. Crises, difficult emotions, haunting loneliness and deep insecurities are daily fare among the clients she assists. Circumstances, explains Barb, often set up situations in which she can speak about the Lord's love and truth for the daily events of living.

The first person Barb led to Christ through her job was the centre's director. As he heard where Barb got her answers to a major life crisis he was wrestling with, he prayed to become a Christian.

"His conversion was the key to my freedom to minister things of the Lord when occasionally deemed imperative, in a supportive program not run by a church organization," said Barb. In the five years since that initial conversion, about twenty Canadian newcomers who passed through the immigration centre have made commitments to Christ, not in a office setting, but rather the result of hours of love, prayer and involvement.

Recently Barb and her husband Denny started a "seekers" Bible study in their home, welcoming an Iraqi Kurd, Muslims, and two Central American couples among the group. One man became a Christian and was baptized at their church. A black South African nominal Christian came to a deeper faith and now fully participates in the church.

In the Lehtos' home congregation, ten of the sixty members are new Canadians who have been loved into the church, and

Barb is optimistic that more Christian growth is on the way. She gives the example of a Muslim family who had been sponsored by a church and lived in Canada for two years before the husband became open to the gospel.

"He came to the conclusion before coming to Canada that Islam did not have the truth," said Barbara. "In befriending this family that I came to really love, I had been open in talking about Jesus Christ, so this man knew where I stood. When he said he wanted to come to church but feared for relatives back home, I invited him instead to church camp. We watched him loosen up and relax to enjoy the fellowship and worship." She asked her women's prayer group to pray for this family.

"We had a strong sense of God's unfolding plan for them from the time they stepped off the plane onto Canadian soil," she said.

She admits that a pitfall of an outreach like she pursues with new Canadians is the risk of "becoming disconnected from the supportive fellowship where we find our own nurture." She and her husband also began to realize that they should not impose expectations of their own ministry onto their church.

"We must not expect our church family to be always johnny-on-the-spot to help when newcomers have needs," she explains. "Not everyone is given the same fitting, zeal, contacts or exposure. But they can be encouraged in learning helping skills, and in the past few years, I've been blessed as my church has become a befriending church to new Canadians."

Bringing Christian love and witness to the families she meets through work is an essential part of how Barb lives out her faith.

"Because it is evident in my work at the centre that I am a Christian, it is essential to develop good working relationships with my partners in the settlement field," Barb emphasizes. "It is important to be competent and professional in all I do, just as it is to admit error and remain vulnerable."

One situation that provoked confrontation involved a Southeast Asian woman who had experienced difficulties with previous pregnancies in refugee camps and wanted an abortion. As every sort of medical support is available in Canada, Barb presented all the other options open to her. This was viewed as interference and an imposition of her Christian values.

"Conflicts like this present a challenge but are necessary," Barb stresses, "for Christians to establish and maintain credibility in the work setting."

■

SHARP IN THE LINE OF DUTY

"Chuck, one thing you have to realize is that you're not normal," one of Chuck Wesley's fellow police officers told him. Normal or not, Chuck finds that the insight he brings to people, both on and off duty, is welcome and useful.

Ontario Provincial Police Sergeant Charles (Chuck) Wesley recently stood and read Psalm 23 beside the bed of a First Nations constable shot in the line of duty. It was part of his job. As staff co-ordinator with the First Nations Police Branch, based in Orillia, Chuck's mandate includes the welfare of First Nations officers.

Professionally, Chuck has to be sensitive to the various religious backgrounds of those he works with. But he is always willing to share his faith when the opportunity arises. When visiting the wounded officer, Chuck noticed a Bible lying on the bed.

Picking it up, he asked if it belonged to the injured man, and discovered that the officer was a Christian. Later, Chuck arranged for other Christian officers to visit the constable, and dropped off some gospel tapes and a cassette player.

Chuck, a striking man in his late forties who is of mixed Cree and English heritage, grew up in the small northern Ontario town of Marathon. He was married there, and joined the OPP twenty-two years ago. Much of his police career has been spent in the Timmins area. His sensitivity to bringing faith into the work place has been a skill he came by the hard way, explains Chuck.

"Initially, if I picked up a person who was intoxicated . . . right away, I'd pull out my New Testament and preach to him, which is really a no-no from my job's perspective." Rather, he finds, he must wait for the other person to ask, or pray that the doors would be opened to naturally, inoffensively share Jesus.

As Chuck's family grew, his concern for his own three sons led him to youth work during his off-duty hours. He wanted his boys to remember him as a man with a Bible, not a beer, in his hand. A talented guitar player and a man with a natural rapport with young people, Chuck helped in youth work at several churches. As he travelled the north, he discovered a youth camp on Lipsett Lake, near Timmins, that had fallen into disuse. Seeing possibilities in the abandoned facility, Chuck contacted his minister. Together with their families they drove to the camp and claimed it for Christ. Ontario's Ministry of Natural Resources sold the camp to Chuck's church, and Camp Katapao was born.

"I've come to realize there is more to being a Christian than just looking after my wife and kids. I have to reach out to other people as well, " explains Chuck.

In his line of work, he has had many experiences of God's

presence. When called on a missing-person search, he prays for the lost person. Chuck remembers one occasion when an elderly woman was lost in the bush near Marathon on a cold night. As Chuck drove the five hours to the search site, he prayed that she would somehow be kept warm. An hour and a half after the search started, the woman was found sitting beside a blazing fire. She told Chuck that she had been freezing at first. Then at about 2 a.m., the time Chuck had been praying, she had reached into her pocket and, even though she was a non-smoker, found a book of matches. Chuck told the woman he had been praying for her.

For Chuck, it is just one example of many that illustrate how God hears and answers prayer in the world of police work.

■

BEYOND PEER PRESSURE

In Fort Nelson, B.C. the junior high school is notorious for its rebellious teenagers. That was bad news for Angela Latham, a Christian since her early childhood, who found herself getting sucked into a world she could see was destroying her.

"I didn't know how to survive in that junior high. I had a really rough time – I lost it. At twelve, thirteen I was drinking, smoking weed," said Angela. "If you weren't in that crowd there wasn't any other to be in. I just wanted to have friends."

She began to fail her classes and, desperate to get out of the situation, she took up an offer from her aunt and uncle to live with them for a while and finish grade nine in Medicine Hat, Alberta.

"I jumped at the chance. I didn't have anything in Nelson that I cared about, nothing really mattered," said Angela. It was a relief to get away from constant arguments with her parents.

She joined a local evangelical church youth group and found herself drawn to those kids, even though they had led a much more sheltered life than she.

"They didn't care who I was pretending to be. They wanted to know who I really was. We didn't have anything in common except Jesus. They really showed me love."

Within the year, Angela had rededicated her life to God.

"As soon as I prayed, I felt a burden lifting off of my back. It was really a drastic change. The temptation to smoke was gone; I held my aunt and uncle's trust and fit much easier into their no-smoking request."

34 —— Beginning to grow in Christ, Angela finished the school year, re-established communication with her parents and returned to her home in Nelson. Within days she was face to face with the drinking, pot-smoking crowd she had escaped from only a few months earlier.

"I was so scared that I ran to my room and prayed. I said 'God, just please be with me. I can't do this on my own.' It got warm in the room and I felt hands on my shoulders – I thought they were angels. I think God was telling me in my heart that He was going to help me, to be there. I'll never forget that day." Strengthened by her pleading encounter in prayer, she knew she had found the strength to avoid what had tempted her so strongly before.

Entering high school in grade nine that season, she found some friends who had become Christians during a revival a few months earlier. Together they formed a youth group and determined to walk in God's truth.

"I learned so much about faith. We would have twenty-four-hour prayer meetings; we would do street witnessing downtown. It was a great time," said Angela.

A year later her whole family moved to Medicine Hat. She enrolled in high school there with a burning passion to share Jesus.

"If you know who you are to God, if you know that Jesus thinks you're wonderful and you know people are dying and going to hell, you want to share," said Angela. She finds opportunities by genuinely asking kids about themselves – how they're doing, if they're happy – and ultimately finds ways to bridge the conversation into talk of Jesus. She invites them to her youth group. Some come, some stay, others just laugh.

Four tough jocks from social studies class laugh when she tells them about God, said Angela. "But you can always tell they're listening and God's Word never returns empty; I know it is sitting in their heart," she said.

One evening she prayed and asked for a special Scripture for the four jocks. She received one for each and wrote it down.

"They didn't tear it up but they did give it back to me. It's like they were afraid to touch it or something. But this one guy, I could tell it meant so much to him that I sneaked it back to him and he put it in his pocket and thanked me."

In the same class on a slow afternoon Angela pulled a small group around her to have a Bible study session. In short time the whole class, including the teacher, had formed a circle around her to hear her explain what the Bible was.

"Anyone can do this if they want to, it's not me talking but Jesus who gives the words. Everyone has the opportunity to witness; all it is an attitude," said Angela.

■

FRIENDSHIP KNOTS

Laurel and Chrystie have been best friends for years. The laughter and loyalty of their friendship began in grade eight, when Laurel introduced Chrystie to her best friend in heaven. With both of them now in post-secondary Christian schools training for ministry, Chrystie reflects on the qualities of a friend she regards as an evangelism hero.

I was attracted to Laurel instantly. She has always been a positive, fun-loving and caring person. Laurel takes a hold of every opportunity to spread God's love. She befriended me when I was all alone in grade eight. That has probably been one of her trademarks – making people feel welcome and appreciated.

At youth group throughout our high school years Laurel was known as the "friendly greeter." She would go to the church half an hour early just so she could greet everyone with a smile and a hug. Whenever new kids came to the group, she was always the first to show them around and make them feel welcome.

It was Laurel's goal to see our group grow by leaps and bounds. At times these newcomers clung to her but she never complained. Even if she had something else to do or was tired of smiling, she never showed it. Her smile is genuine and it comes from the heart, not the mouth.

Laurel took on the task of being on our high school Christian fellowship committee for two years. She planned the Tuesday Bible studies and many of the events. While she was there, the group reached record-breaking numbers. I am convinced this was because of Laurel's special touch and love for those around her.

Even in the little things Laurel let her light shine. She worked at McDonald's in grade nine. Her main motivation for taking the job was to meet non-Christians and, through her example, prayers and words, witness to them. Everyone working there knew where

Laurel stood in her spiritual life and that God was her number one priority.

Laurel decided to go to a Bible school not far from home after high school. She was thrilled when people would ask what her after-graduation plans were. This gave her a perfect opportunity to tell them about why she would go to a Bible school. To Laurel there was a witnessing opportunity behind every door.

I don't know how many people have been affected by Laurel. I believe it would be too many to count. I do know, that without her in my life, I would not be who I am today. She is a woman who constantly lets God lead her, and as a result He has given her wonderful gifts. I cannot thank Him enough for this treasure.

—— 37

■

ACADEMIC FREEDOM

When Dr. Bruce Wilkinson stands in front of 500 students in his introductory economics class every September, he talks about more than exams and essays; he tells the students he is a follower of Jesus. Bruce, who has a PhD in economics, has taught at the University of Alberta since 1967. Every introductory class in those twenty-seven years has heard about his dedication to Jesus Christ.

"I know that some of my colleagues tell their students they don't believe in God, so I think it's just as fair to share my belief," the professor explains. "I like to let my students know that Jesus is a vital part of my life and that that affects my outlook as an economist. We all have a perspective, and that's mine."

Bruce does not fear the reactions of the students. At end-of-term professor evaluations, he usually receives only one or two critical comments about his shared Christianity.

"Students often come up to me and thank me. One student said he appreciated my talking about Jesus because in his math class the professor talked about not believing in God."

Bruce, raised as a Christian, dedicated his life to God when he was ten. His Christian walk has been fairly straightforward, without any major periods of rebellion. A 1971 sabbatical in England with his wife was a significant turning point for him.

"It was a great time of real renewal for us. We were attending an evangelical Anglican Church . . . and we developed a new, deeper relationship with Jesus."

Three years ago he heard a Youth With A Mission member speak on prayer; that got Bruce thinking about starting up something at the university.

"I talked to a few Christian colleagues, who talked to others and saw that some people wanted to be involved."

The result has been thirty-five University of Alberta staff members praying in small groups weekly.

"There are all denominations – Catholic, Anglican, Baptist, Pentecostal, Christian Reform, Mennonite. Nobody worries about denominations."

They pray for the university, students, colleagues and personal needs.

"I find it absolutely vital. Prayer is the most important aspect of my life – without Jesus there's no meaning. I certainly say it's been strengthening to me and to the others."

Bruce is able to turn all kinds of situations into opportunities to share about Christ. When students come into his office

requesting extensions on papers, he finds that a golden opportunity.

"If students aren't doing well in their courses I usually find
there's some sort of a problem in their lives. I use it as an occasion
to ask, 'How's your relationship with God?' That opens it up right
up. Some might say, 'I don't know who God is.' And then I share
with them."

As a result, some students have become Christians.

"About two years ago a girl talked to me. She was having a really tough time at home. I shared with her and she accepted Christ."
Following up, Bruce found that she had bought a Bible and
become involved with a church.

Bruce once received in the mail a picture of a man being baptized in the Pacific Ocean.

"He wrote that he had been in my international trade class. He — 39
wrote, 'You talked about Jesus and I thought you were nuts.' " But
as that former student was trekking through the Himalayas he ran
into people who talked about Jesus and he remembered Bruce's
words.

"There are other little examples too," Bruce noted quietly. He
went to see a singing group at a church one evening and the
youth pastor approached him. He said he had been in Bruce's
class and that he did not believe in God until then. Now he is a
youth pastor.

"It encourages me to see these things happen."

Bruce also talks to colleagues about Christ.

"I have a standard answer I use for people who have turned from
Christianity as the result of what someone else has done. I say that if
you were studying chemistry and somebody said take two parts
hydrogen and one part oxygen to make water and something went
wrong and the test tube blew up – would you throw away the chem-

istry book? No, you wouldn't. I'd say they didn't follow the book.

"And the same goes with Christianity – the person hasn't followed the book. I've used that with PhDs and they say, 'I've never thought of that.' "

■

HIV Positive

"Every day that I'm on the street, at least one acquaintance tells me he is HIV positive," said Claude Trottier sadly. Once a freedom-seeker in the hippie culture of California, Claude has given his heart and life to sharing the freedom Jesus gives with homosexuals, drug addicts and prostitutes in Montreal.

40 ——— "We can barely walk a block without someone coming to see him about their needs or to say hello," said a friend of Claude Trottier. "The keys to Claude's successful ministry are trust and friendship."

It has been a long journey that led Claude to his present call to live and work for the gospel in the gay village of Montreal. In 1970, at the age of twenty-one, disillusioned with family and other relationships, Claude headed for Berkeley, California and the promised love of the hippie movement. Step by step, God brought him to a clear understanding of the gospel. Eventually, he found himself in Boulder, Colorado, staying in a house run by the Navigators. After many weeks of persistent and loving discussion, his Navigator friend led him to a saving knowledge of Jesus.

For several years, Claude remained with the Navigators. Later he returned to Quebec to join their new evangelistic ministry in Quebec City, and began to seek answers to some of the deeper questions of spirituality and sexuality. At the same time, he realized how deep his compassion and understanding were for the suffering of marginal people – people like he was at one time: the punks, drug users and homosexuals.

This questioning eventually led Claude to Youth With A Mission (YWAM), where he worked with marginal people in the inner core of Amsterdam in the mid-1980s. Then he stepped back from ministry for a time of learning and spiritual restoration through a process of inner healing, later returning to Montreal, to work with YWAM there.

For the past two years in Montreal, YWAM (Jeunesse en Mission) and Operation Mobilization have made a concerted effort to reach young male and female prostitutes, drug users, punks, street kids and homosexuals in the gay village.

Claude has already lived in the village for two years. Part of his strategy is to befriend many in the community and to be there for — 41 them in times of need. He never has to wait long, as the suicide rate, the numbers of HIV-positive people and the brothel atmosphere keep thousands living on the edge of despair.

"Every day that I'm on the street at least one acquaintance tells me he's HIV positive," Claude said sadly.

Claude and his team are deeply respected by the community, though they have felt like apprentices in this draining ministry for the past two years.

"This is not for a new Christian," he said, "and [it's] only for someone whom God has specifically called."

The team has a clear vision and each member is accountable to the others. They spend extended times in prayer and Bible study together to combat the spiritual forces they sense.

"This is a front-line ministry," said Claude. "We're often the targets for Satan's attacks."

Although Claude is an evangelist and can talk to anyone on the street about Christ in a natural way, he and the team have also chosen another approach. They have become volunteers in various social services extended to the community by the city. They serve in centres for drug addicts and people with AIDS, providing a listening ear and practical services. This can range from housekeeping to bringing food and preparing meals.

Claude is also the director of Info-Action SIDA (SIDA is French for AIDS). This is a Christian network of trained volunteers who minister to people with AIDS. Because of the excellent training the volunteers receive, it has been recognized by the city as an official social service.

There are many ups and downs to Claude's work. One nineteen-year-old whom Claude had befriended for three years and who had not responded to the gospel ended his life in suicide. It is at times like that that Claude feels the most pain. He listens to people's stories of abuse in the home and the crises they have lived through. Many are dying of AIDS. Although they reach out to him in raw need, many turn away from God and His message.

On the other hand, Claude specifically seeks those who are new in the neighbourhood.

"You can usually spot them," he said. "They have a brighter look in their eyes. They haven't been too tarnished yet." He takes them aside and gives them a reality check on the real nature of the village. When these young guys realize that what they thought would be an adventure and a quick buck is really a brothel of promiscuity leading to death, they often will turn away the same day and head home fast. Some tell Claude that they know it was not an accident that they met him upon arriving in the village. This is one of the rewards of Claude's work. In many small ways, he sees God's hand at work in people's lives. This keeps him going.

Thanks to the "gracious solitude" God has designed for Claude's life as a single man, he spends many hours in God's presence in prayer and building his spiritual resources from the Bible. He especially appreciates his director Pierre Lebel's ministry to him in helping maintain his perspective in times of frustration.

The word of the Lord that came to him at the start of his ministry continues to direct his vision. God had told him He would take him back to his own ghetto and that the Lord his redeemer would make a "way in the desert and streams in the wasteland" (Isaiah 43:19).

For this "desert" calling to the gay village, Claude said, "I am at peace with the God of love."

■

KIDS, COOKS, COUNSELLORS

Dorothy Currie started Bible clubs in the basement of her Saskatoon home as a young mother thirty-seven years ago. Since then she has seen more than 1,000 children come and go, many of them making decisions for Jesus, and the rest taking with them the seeds of the experience.

"There are so many hurting little kids out there these days, somebody's got to tell them that they love them, and that the Lord loves them," says seventy-three-year-old Dorothy Currie. "I just can't tell you how many little hurting ones there are out there; my heart aches for them."

Her love for the children of Saskatchewan is as vast as the prairie sky. In the winter months she hosts home Bible clubs for children; in the summer she spends six weeks travelling around the province's church camps, conducting chapels for the children and devotions for the cooks and counsellors.

"I'm at these camps because I feel our time is short and I just said to the Lord, 'You give me the health, and I'll go,' " said Dorothy during an interview in the motorhome her husband Ken bought to help her on her summer camp circuit. With a warm sun shadow-dappling the leaves outside the camper, she cuddled her toy poodle A.J. and spoke about her years of home Bible club.

"I have moms come to my Bible club that used to attend themselves at one time. Our son . . . [Dr. Dave Currie, an Abbotsford, B.C. youth pastor] . . . is thirty-nine. He was two when I started.

"When I hear him give his testimony of how he became a Christian, standing beside the piano at the Bible club . . . he said he was seven . . . it's worth it, for just my son."

On Mondays and Tuesdays after school children and moms troop down to Dorothy's basement for an hour of singing, stories and Bible study.

"The children invite each other, Dorothy said. "They bring their friends. Children can bring children easier than I can go out and bring them in."

The mothers sit at the end of the rumpus room with their coffee; Dorothy sets up her elaborate flannelgraph boards and the eager children sit on the floor in front. Mothers invite other mothers and their children as well, and generally these are from unchurched families.

"So they all get in on the Bible verses, the singing. . . . The moms get in on that too."

But like many other things, the Bible clubs are falling victim to the age, Dorothy said.

"Many years ago there weren't all the Nintendos and all this going on." Last year enrolment was about twenty, but years ago it was more like forty. "It's just harder to get kids nowadays — there are so many other things they're involved in."

The years of her involvement have brought tears as well as joy. Several years ago a ten-year-old girl from her Bible club was at a riding academy and fell from her horse and was killed.

"I still remember the day I went over to see this distraught mother. I could never believe it. . . . [It's so painful] when your little one is taken like that. . . .

"But the little girl had made a commitment. I believe she's with the Lord. She memorized all the verses and made a decision for Christ. And through this ministry her mother now attends our neighbourhood Bible study."

Dorothy likes to think that a lot of my kids are living for the Lord, "but I can't say as they are." So many have passed through her clubs that she cannot keep track of them. She clings to the Lord's promise, "Train a child . . . and when he is old he will not turn from it" Proverbs 22:6.

"I just keep thinking on things like that. These kids are trained. When they're old they'll come back."

■

RIGHT IDEAS FOR THE RIGHT TIME

People who have the ability to come up with the right idea not only at the right time but often just minutes ahead of everyone else are amazing. What traits tend to characterize these people? They listen carefully to what others are saying, maintain a close walk with the Lord and stay aware of the big picture around them.

Summed up in a word, it is a matter of perspective. Our world can become cluttered with competing and distracting noises and images. With all that pressure, it does not take much for us to lose our perspective on what it is that God really wants us to do.

Take Nehemiah, for instance. While he is listening to his close family and friends, he recognizes the need for the walls of Jerusalem to be rebuilt, which, in the big picture, was certainly important. Not wanting to be mistaken, Nehemiah takes the apparent need to God, seeking His face in worship and confession and reminding Him of His promises. It is here in prayer that the action plan is conceived, resulting in the right idea for the right time. Nehemiah courageously approaches the King and is successful in obtaining safe passage and the provisions essential for the fulfilment of his God-given plan. Recognizing God's hand on Nehemiah's plan, God's people rally with a spirit of commitment and cooperation to accomplish the task fifty-two days later in spite of enemy opposition. Nehemiah became the man of the hour because of his ability to listen to God and keep matters in perspective. The full account of his story is found in Nehemiah 1-6.

— 49

All the people in the following stories sensed what God wanted them to do and when to do it. In some cases their actions were unprecedented and in other cases they were inspired by other people or programs for the specific steps they took. In every story you will find an undeniable dependence on the Lord and the guidance of His Spirit.

– dm

FROM

ANOTHER

PERSPECTIVE

So if you're serious about living this new resurrection life with Christ, act like it. Pursue the things over which Christ presides. Don't shuffle along, eyes to the ground, absorbed with the things right in front of you. Look up, and be alert to what is going on around Christ – that's where the action is. See things from his perspective.

Colossians 3 (TM)

HE SHOOTS — HE SCORES

If God could use a hockey coach to draw Bobby Dunn to salvation,
Bobby thought there might be a future in using the sport as a ministry tool.
Now every summer Bobby and his early coach Allan Andrews see
hundreds of kids pass through a hockey camp on Prince Edward Island
where Jesus is part of the team.

Bobby Dunn was not sure where his life was going in 1980 when he decided to start praying about it. He was not a Christian, but he knew where he could find one.

"Something inside me said 'Go ask Allan Andrews,' " recalled Bobby, now thirty-five. A few months later, Allan led him to the Lord.

Allan Andrews had been Bobby's hockey coach and friend when he was in school. "I knew he was kind of religious because when we played hockey he would have us bow our heads and pray before a game."

"Any time I coached over the years, we always had a quiet time before they went on the ice," Allan explained. "I think the Lord takes the little things you do and multiplies them."

Bobby credits Allan with a quiet witness that has drawn not just him but numerous young hockey players, parents and coaches to the Christian faith. The two now work together in a sports training school run by Allan that brings some 1,200 kids from all over Canada to Summerside, Prince Edward Island each summer.

"He's an influencer," said Bobby. "He befriends you in a quiet way."

"I try to live my life and be available," said Allan, fifty-three. "People know there's something different about you when you're a Christian." That availability meant writing letters and talking on the phone when Bobby had questions about the Christian faith.

Allan lets potential students and instructors know from the outset what his values are. His letterhead quotes Psalm 127:3: Children "are a heritage from the Lord."

"We look at kids as valuable human beings," Allan explained. "We use a lot of positive reinforcement."

"He makes you feel good about yourself," Bobby pointed out. Bobby remembers a friend who was having trouble finishing high school. "Allan made him believe in himself." That friend eventually completed a master's degree in criminology and joined the Philadelphia Flyers. And when he began to think about the meaning of life, "the Lord put Allan in his path and a couple of years later he gave his life to the Lord."

Many of the instructors Allan has hired over the years have also come to a personal faith in Christ. A couple of years ago one of them was drinking to the extent that it affected his work. Allan took him aside and spoke frankly to him. Bobby, who is the school's director of training and development, kept the man on staff despite his irresponsibility. Bobby took him to hear a Christian singer, and he accepted the Lord. Last summer the instructor came back to the school, his life changed. He thanked Allan for his help.

Although the hockey school is not a Christian organization, the fact that Allan, Bobby and some of the other staff are Christians has a big impact on how it is run.

"It's more than just a hockey school," Bobby explained. "There's a big emphasis on lifestyle." Each week includes a session on lifestyle and values. Instructors explain to the students how choices lead to habits, how habits build character, how character affects relationships, and how relationships affect lifestyles. "We emphasize lifestyle as much as we do hockey skills."

Instructors receive training, too. Orientation sessions before the hockey schools begin include an emphasis on being a role model.

"Because of the modelling that goes on, you don't hear bad jokes or bad language," said Bobby.

Allan is always clear where he stands but waits for the right opportunity before talking to people directly about the Lord. His relationship often starts with offering a book on Christianity and athletics or inviting someone to his home. Last summer the mother of one of the boys trying out for a team was in a bad accident and ended up in hospital. Allan visited her and suggested a book she might like to read.

"Paul said he earned the right [to witness] by becoming all things to all people. I think you've got to be friends to them, relate to what they like, show an interest in what they're interested in."

Then the opportunities to talk will come, he says.

And underlying his friendships is this fact: "The Lord loves people more than we do. If you make yourself available, that's all He asks for."

— 53

■

H APPY H OUR A FTER F OUR

Years ago, Happy Hour in Swan River, Manitoba meant spending an hour with a woman who loved Jesus. Edith Krumm, now eighty-four, has since found new ways to repackage her desire to reach children for Jesus. Her story is told through the eyes of Ruby Schell. Since 1933, Ruby has been blessed by the witness of "The Happy Hour Lady".

From day one, Edith has been a dynamo hauling kids to and from Sunday school. In fact, she is now bringing the grandchildren of her first recruits to Sunday school. Edith married and raised four children, and she also taught school as a grade one teacher. This was before social assistance was available, and Edith's heart broke for the needs and poverty of her students. Many of these were native children and Edith decided to do something. Convincing a neighbour to lend her basement for a Bible study, Edith began "Happy Hour After Four."

Some thirty children attended, with Edith making several car trips to the nearby reserve. Edith also taught Sunday school and AWANA (a church children's club program) for many years and has faithfully witnessed to her own children, even having the joy of leading little grandchildren to Christ.

Now, at eighty-four, Edith is taking full advantage of the Manitoba government's provisions that allow for voluntary religious instruction after school. This year, twenty-four children signed up for Edith's class, and all of them said yes to following Jesus as a result of opportunities presented in her teaching time.

Edith would tell you she has not done much and that she really does not know if her work has done any good. But just the other day Edith's niece phoned from Winnipeg to get a special date from her Auntie Edith. It was a time when Edith took the girl to hear an evangelist and, unknown to Edith, her niece accepted Christ at that time.

Years later, this niece still marks that evening with Auntie Edith as her beginning in the kingdom of Christ.

In my church at Little Woody, we have three generations of families in which Edith Krumm was the implement in directing them to service for the Lord today.

Edith is still my hero.

■

CULTURE SHOCK

Glen Povey understands culture shock, not only by observation but by participation. His heart for ministry to Canada's urban natives prompted him to move his family into a predominantly native section of Regina and work at developing community there.

Glen Povey got his first glimpse of racism in his teens when his family offered to care for a young native boy whose mother had been diagnosed with cancer. Bringing a native person into the family was an eye opener. Glen soon found his classmates treating him differently. He saw how unfair discrimination is.

Much later, while in university, Glen became a Christian through the testimony of a fellow student, and the idea of native ministry began to stir in his heart. After graduation, believing God was calling him to work with natives, he returned to Regina, went to seminary, and began teaching in inner city schools. He taught for five years, building relationships with the families of his native students.

Then he moved his family into a predominantly native area of the city and began home Bible studies. These grew so much that he took a wall out of his home to accommodate thirty people at a time. Still the studies kept growing.

Seven years ago the fellowship began to rent a vacant church in the neighbourhood. The new congregation, with Glen as pastor, eventually purchased and renovated the building, and now attendance averages 100 on Sundays. The members of Morning Star church give generously and sacrificially from low incomes, providing a modest salary for their pastor. The church receives no direct support from a denomination. It's a real challenge for the congregation, Glen says, but a healthy one.

The Poveys' lifestyle as a family speaks as much as their words. The oldest of three daughters spent the summer learning Spanish while doing volunteer work in Central America. In the past Glen's wife has supplemented the income by teaching part-time at a Christian school. This year the church is starting its own Christian school to meet the needs of many families in the congregation. That means she will have a new job – albeit one that does not pay.

Native people who move to the city experience serious culture shock. In a desperate attempt to cope with city life, they often turn to drugs and alcohol. One of their greatest needs is for a strong sense of community – a supportive environment for themselves and their families. Glen believes the best way for them to cope is within a community of native people who know the ropes, people who have coped successfully and can now serve as role models. To that end he works at nurturing people who have leadership ability. He has become something of a catalyst, creating community within a culture that is not his own.

56 ——— Five years ago, Glen felt God leading him to reach out by going door to door to every native family in Regina. With back issues of *Indian Life*, a Christian magazine directed toward natives, in hand he set about his task.

One door he knocked on was that of a prostitute. She was angry, but took the magazine and his card.

"If ever you want to get out of the lifestyle you're in, give me a call," Glen told her.

Several months later she phoned. After some rough experiences on the street she came to the Poveys' home and made a sincere commitment to Christ. She also put her three kids in Christian schools and went on to study nursing. After graduation she returned to her old neighbourhood to work as a street nurse. She now attends Bible school.

Another home visit brought Glen in contact with a man who had found faith in Christ while in jail for a murder conviction. The ex-convict was now living with a woman and six children.

Glen's visit helped him decide to recommit his life to God. He began attending Morning Star church and attended Bible school for four years. He has since married the woman he was living with, and is assistant pastor of the church.

Morning Star now runs a "Love Bus" – a travelling coffee house that goes each week to bars, house parties, fights or to the downtown core where drug dealers are active. On board are former prostitutes, pimps and drug addicts who share with people in trouble – many of them friends from their former lifestyle.

For Glen, it is exciting to share the gospel with people whose lives are in desperate condition. With little of the sophistication, facades or masks that are common in middle class society, the people in the inner city know their lives are moving quickly to a dead end. Seeing lives and families transformed is, in Glen's words, "a wonderfully rewarding thing."

— 57

■

A ROOF OVERHEAD

When Luke and Anne Stack began looking for an opportunity to serve Christ in a more tangible way five years ago, they stumbled across a 107-unit apartment complex and a desperate need for single-parent housing.

Luke and Anne Stack were garden-variety Christians who wanted to be involved in active ministry, but had no formal training. So they looked for what they could do with what they did have.

"We had met with many single parents who seemed to be in dire straits looking for housing, so we felt that this would be an excellent opportunity," Luke explained. Having been raised in a single-parent home, he knew about the very practical needs.

Shortly after the Stacks formed the Society of Housing Opportunities and Progressive Employment (HOPE), a public housing complex became available. With the cooperation of the Canada Mortgage and Housing Corporation, the society took over management of the facility and designed twenty-five subsidized housing units for single parents.

Not only did this provide affordable places for the families, but it also allowed Luke to work full-time as the executive director of the Society of HOPE.

"That was a real miracle," he recalled. "Getting those buildings was God's blessing, because it opened the doors in a big way."

Since then the society has expanded with the addition of a facility known as the Hope House. With the help of the Stacks' home church and a variety of other local churches, a grant from the City of Kelowna and some additional fund-raising, the society renovated a heritage home in the downtown area. This provided three extra units, primarily for single mothers to come to in times of need. The work has received positive public reaction. Support has come not only from the churches, but from the city council and community as well.

The goal of the ministry is to physically assist those in need, but the society also desires to meet the spiritual needs of people, who typically come from troubled backgrounds. As Luke describes it, "We don't evangelize as a society but we do try and lay the groundwork for the church. It's a very fine line."

He makes it clear that HOPE is not a church or directly linked to a church, but its staff simply desire to provide a service to people.

"When asked why we do it, we respond by saying, 'We do it because we believe Jesus wants us to.' "

In the past few years, the Stacks have seen their work make a real difference in the lives of these single parents.

"We've seen five or six ladies come to the Lord over the past two years," Luke said. He recalls a day he met a woman at a Bible study who had just come from a broken marriage. The society managed to find her an apartment in the building. Shortly after that, she gave her life to the Lord, and within a year was able to get her marriage back together. She has since become a member of the Society of HOPE and serves in a leadership capacity.

Unfortunately, for every happy ending there are usually three or four others that do not work out so well. But Luke and Anna know that even though it is not always easy, they take the Bible seriously when it says, "Religion that God our Father accepts as pure and faultless is this: to look after orphans and widows in their distress." (James 1:27 NIV)

■

D OUBT AND D EBATE

On staff with Intervarsity Christian Fellowship (IVCF), John Bowen had spent more than ten years in the work of training leaders, teaching Bible studies and giving Christian care to university students. By the late 1980s, he felt something was starting to go wrong.

I was becoming bored with my work. I was still doing it as well as I knew how, but for some reason my heart was moving on: where, I did not know.

Then I read Scott Peck's book *The Road Less Travelled*. What particularly struck me was Peck's thesis that we grow only through change, that change means leaving behind what is familiar and comfortable – and that it is risky.

That was it. I was not changing, not growing, taking no risks.

There was no urgency to my praying. I almost felt I could have done my job as well if God had not existed. Something had to change.

For reasons I am not sure of even now, the idea emerged that I would deliver a weekly series of lectures entitled "Ten Myths About Christianity" in a high traffic area of Carleton University in Ottawa, where hundreds of students walked through every lunch time. With one or two students' help we booked the space, set out publicity, arranged two rows of chairs, and – I did it. Not many people stopped to listen; not many Christian students took an interest; but for me it was a liberation. Maybe God was trying to tell me something.

The following year, a high school group I was working with was discussing what they could do as a major outreach event in the school. I ran over some of the things I had seen other groups do, "or you could do a debate," I ended. They loved the idea and I could even suggest an atheistic speaker who would enthusiastically argue the non-existence of God. But what about a Christian speaker? They discussed this for a few minutes, but I knew what I had to say. I could almost feel the Holy Spirit breathing down my neck, saying, "Well . . . ?" Finally, I surrendered. "I suppose maybe I could do that." That settled it.

We did the debate. More than 500 students came out and that was good enough for me. With some trembling, I said, "Okay, Lord, what's the next risk?"

I talked this over with friends and one, experienced in career counselling, said, "Write down what's in your heart. What is it that you really, really want to do ?"

I recall what I wrote that fall of 1990 and it is still true:

"I have a powerful internal urge to talk to people about God. I long to help them see how it makes sense to believe in the Christian God.

Helping people to see is the key, I think. People cannot be reasoned into the kingdom, though reason is a part of it: they have to see it. And the way they see (apart from the work of the Spirit) is by having word pictures painted for them which put together the elements of life as they experience it, in a way that shows God to be the hidden focus of all they know and experience."

Shortly after that, Rosemary Green came to Ottawa, to do a prayer seminar. One of her exercises was to see if maybe God would speak to us through whatever happened to be in our pockets. Two days after the seminar, I thought I would try Rosemary's idea. As soon as I began to feel in my pocket, I knew what I would find and smiled. In my pocket was a roll of film on its way to be developed.

I am the film; God is both photographer and camera. Inside me there is darkness until God exposes his light onto the light-sensitive surface inside. Those impressions of God's light remain on my film and I want to share those pictures with others. No one else has quite the pictures I do. I cherish them as gifts from God and I know they can be helpful to other people.

The film-in-my-pocket lesson showed me I had to choose a career path. As I proposed the idea of a professional debate ministry, my supervisor said, "You realize we may not know for five years whether this will work or not." I was grateful that he had the faith to wait that long.

Now, when unchurched students say to me things like, "Wow, this is amazing. I never knew Christianity was this interesting," or "I feel as though God is becoming real to me," I know I made the right choice. My photographs are communicating.

■

Rethinking Community

Bob Walker is turning his life upside down to pick on a deeply held Canadian habit: autonomous living. Your home, eating habits and even weekly chores would be changed if Walker had his way. He is a thirty-two-year-old property developer and graduate student in Toronto, active in two different co-housing groups as a means to help win his world for Christ.

When it comes to sharing the gospel, Bob Walker thinks communally and globally. He sees faith as redeeming not only individuals but whole neighbourhoods, cities, and cultures. His vision of Christianity is one of an alive, pulsating faith that tears down the boundaries set up by modern nuclear suburban homes, privatized religion and fellowship once or twice a week.

"We need to think about re-structuring the way people actually live in order to make our faith less individualistic and private," explained Bob. "Unless we examine the premise of modern society, especially its individualism, we will forever be inventing techniques to save souls for the after-life, rather than getting down to the difficult business of being sanctified, making disciples and showing the world what a redeemed humanity looks like. Christ called us to have all areas of lives under His lordship and this means living radically different from those who bow before other gods."

Bob believes that Christ's lordship will change the structures that govern how we live our daily lives.

"The layout of our suburbs, the design of our neighbourhoods, the primacy of the car, the requirement to travel to have fellowship with other Christians, and the delegation of an incredibly large number of tasks to the government, all have certain views of being human underlying them," said Bob. "By accepting Jesus as lord of all of life, we must make sure that the way we live in those structures corresponds to the way He has called us to live."

Bob asserts that one of the first things most Christians need is more community built into their lives. The way to solve this, according to Bob, is not to send people to church more frequently, but rather to send the church to them. That is to say, fellowship with other Christians should be built right into the fabric of everyday life; it should not be something which one must travel to or make an appointment for.

Bob believes Christians can enjoy this fellowship and also be living witnesses to others who do not, in a new residential community design called cohousing.[1] Developed in Denmark more than twenty-five years ago, this little-known phenomenon is basically an intentional neighbourhood planned by the residents and physically designed to facilitate interaction.

Cohousing strikes a healthy balance between private and public space. It is not a commune, which Bob feels destroys individuality; neither is it modern autonomy, which he says undermines community and a proactive, "this-worldly" faith.

—— 63

In these communities, families are kept together and can live completely self-sufficiently in their own dwellings; but at the same time, the home design discourages isolation by the close proximity of other neighbours, by the shared facilities and the green space in the pedestrian friendly courtyard. A typical complex consists of

---

[1] The term cohousing was coined by Kathryn McCamand and Charles Durrett in 1988 with their landmark book *Cohousing: A Contemporary Approach to Housing Ourselves* (Berkeley, Calif: Ten Speed Press, 1988). This husband-and-wife team of architects introduced this neighbourhood design into North America. Since the book came out there have been hundreds of groups formed in North America, with six projects completed, approximately eleven more in process, and twenty-five other groups searching for suitable land. Bob's project is believed to be the first of its kind in Ontario.

thirty families of all types and sizes occupying about three acres, with parking on the periphery and the homes in a horseshoe pattern facing into the people-friendly interior. In the middle of it all is the common house where the large eating area, laundry, play rooms exercise rooms, mail boxes, etc. are located.

What makes these communities work effectively is 1) the interaction required by the group to plan and design their community prior to construction, 2) the voluntary community meals in the evenings and 3) facilities which are designed to promote neighbourliness.

Within the concept, Bob believes that evangelism and gospel-living opportunities are greatly enhanced. He stresses that such communities should not be 100 percent Christian. The point, he says, is to increase quality, in-depth relationships with Christians and non-Christians, not to cloister oneself off in a secluded utopia.

Yet if Bob is successful in getting his dream lifestyle evangelism project off the ground in north suburban Toronto where he has targeted it for in spring of 1996, it does sound like a utopic living.

You would raise your children in a place where you trusted everyone. You would come home from a hard day at the office and find a meal prepared for you.[2] On the spur of the moment you could play cards with some neighbours; you would watch your children become increasingly disinterested in TV because of the constant supply of other kids and activities.

---

[2] In the typical thirty-family cohousing complex, with two adults making supper five days a week, it works out that one has to cook only once every four weeks. The time saving is enormous and this feature of cohousing is the most universally praised and used. Of course, if a family wants to cook in their own kitchen that is fine too, but few elect to do that on a regular basis.

And what if some of these neighbours were people you could pray with, or were elderly saints who could disciple you, or who could keep you accountable? Or what if there was a guest room in the common house set aside for people in need?

As Bob shares his enthusiastic vision with the curious, he prays that Canada's churched community will be open to this radical restructuring. He is convinced that only by careful examination of the way we live, and by consequent change will we be able to lead western culture out of darkness. He believes this holistic gospel, which refuses to separate evangelism, discipleship or societal renewal, must win the day if Christians are to incarnate God's truth to this generation.

"It will take more than co-housing to redeem society," Bob acknowledged. "But this step alone will begin to make Christianity the counter-culture many people are searching for, and not the unfortunate subculture it has become."

— 65

THE SPIRIT'S
NUDGE

Although it was still early in the morning, the family had gone their various ways and Glen knelt to pray for tough needs of the native population of his city. He struggled with the apparent inability of the government, social agencies and churches to make a significant impact. As he began to pray he heard a noise at the back door. Irritated that he could not get down to prayer, he went to check it out. He found a familiar person reading and recording the figures from the utility meter. Since he was already interrupted, Glen struck up a conversation and discovered it took an amazingly few people to read the more than 40,000 residential meters in the city.

Returning to his room and his knees for prayer, Glen's mind was still fascinated by the numbers and how easy it appeared for such a massive task to be accomplished. Then in prayer the idea came that he could undertake a massive task to reach the native — 69 community in a very practical way.

Within weeks, he had a generous supply of the attractive, native-written magazine entitled *Indian Life*. He began knocking on doors of native homes and offering a free copy of the magazine if they would promise to read it and take time to discuss it on his return. To his surprise, it did not take long before he had distributed hundreds of copies and had wonderful opportunities of sitting in native homes listening to concerns and responding with the message of the gospel. Bible studies were begun and today there is a new native church in that city, largely emerging out of this humble beginning.

Was the knock at the door during Glen's time of prayer coincidence or was it the nudge of the Holy Spirit, leading Glen to an inspired idea?

Every story in this chapter bears the mark of that characteristic. In each story, by His Spirit, God has spoken to individuals giving them a vision of what He wants them to do in response to significant needs in their worlds. The quality time each person has spent in the Word of God and prayer has provided an ongoing responsiveness to His Spirit when He nudges. In fact, the evidence is clear that the more time one spends developing a relationship with our Heavenly Father the more clearly He speaks into one's life providing clarity of vision and strategy. As you look into the face of Jesus, it does not take long before you realize how much you need to change in order to be like Him. Confession takes place and the change process begins. You begin to recognize His nudges as never before.

As His vision for you unravels, more often than not there is a strong relationship to your past faith pilgrimage, your spiritual giftedness, your abilities, your spheres of influence and the countless other dynamics in your life which He has sovereignly woven into the fabric of your life. The more time you spend with Him the more opportunities He will have to communicate to you the special ways you can convey His Son's unconditional love to a needy world.

– dm

70 ——

FROM

ANOTHER

PERSPECTIVE

By entering through faith into what God has always wanted to do for us . . . We throw open our doors to God and discover at the same moment that he has already thrown open his door to us. We find ourselves standing where we always hoped we might stand — out in the wide open spaces of God's grace and glory, standing tall and shouting our praise . . . We can't round up enough containers to hold everything God generously pours into our lives through the Holy Spirit.

Romans 5 (TM)

HIGH-TECH CARRIER

No matter where he is — on a plane, at a business meeting, in his
condominium complex, or in another country — Jack Klemke seems
to find ways of sharing his faith with others. He is a man with a unique
ability to make God real to people.

Every day, Alberta businessman Jack Klemke starts by asking
God to help him be sensitive to the open doors waiting for him.
That availability and close relationship with God, he explains, is
the key to opening doors to sharing his faith with other people.

"It's not complicated. It's pretty simple," he said. "You walk in
the Spirit and live in the Spirit. It seems to me that always has to
be the starting point."

Jack, who now heads the business he started with his father
forty-five years ago, has found those doors opening both in his
neighbourhood and in international circles. He and his wife Carol
have spent time praying for the people in the building where they
live. One Easter, along with other Christian couples in the complex, they introduced themselves to their neighbours, offering
them copies of the *Jesus* video produced by Campus Crusade for
Christ.

Now a popular tool in Canada and worldwide (the film has
been translated into more than 300 languages, with another 135
in progress) the *Jesus* film holds special meaning for Jack — his
interest in the project goes back to its pre-production days.

The advent of technology that has allowed communication systems like never before gives Christians living in the 1990s a
unique opportunity to share the gospel, Jack says. Satellites, faxes,
telephones and delivery systems all make communication quicker
and more efficient than ever.

"I think God allowed the development of all that technology
for such a time as this," he reflected.

But, he is quick to add, sophisticated technology is no substitute for personal evangelism and discipleship. Jack has had a hand in establishing training centres in several countries to teach people how to share their faith.

A few decades ago, the Klemkes were not as keen on expressing their personal beliefs to people they met. Then a neighbour said to Jack's wife, "You're so busy with your church." That realization, and allowing the Holy Spirit to work in his life, helped Jack to grow in his ability – and desire – to share with others.

Keenly interested in what is happening in different parts of the world, Jack has been involved in organizing dinners, seminars and other events for government officials, diplomats and business people, both in Canada and in their home countries.

"They need Christ like the rest of us," he pointed out. Working with teams of Christians through various agencies, primarily Campus Crusade for Christ, he helps make contact with a specific group, and looks for creative ways to present the gospel to them. "The key is to ask the Lord to help us be creative," he said.

That combination of creativity and guidance by the Holy Spirit is effective. A former member of the Russian Parliament, among others, has accepted Christ and is being discipled. His life has turned around.

Not everyone has the opportunity to move in an international community. But Jack suggests that opportunities exist no matter where we live. Christians in any city or town in Canada can relate to their Member of Parliament, provincial government representative, school trustee or municipal councillor, he says.

"Start with prayer, and as the opportunity presents itself, get involved in meaningful dialogue. I think that's where we'll see societal change."

"KID, WHY'RE YOU DOING THIS?"

*Living with and talking about Jesus comes naturally in the Turton house-
hold of Kitchener, Ontario, where Matthew, eleven, bicycles around the
neighbourhood with a Christian message, composing songs and skits to take
to local seniors and nursing homes.*

I like to tell what God does. He's done so much for me. I'm not
supposed to have been born because of my mom's back. But I'm
here, praise God! For the first four years of my life, I had a life-
threatening condition called malabsorption, that meant food went
out of me almost as quick as it was put in. Mom had to carry a lot
of food around for me whenever we were out, because I was always
hungry. I wasn't really great to have on the social scene either,
because I had to wear diapers all the time. I remember the celebration of my first birthday after God healed me. I had chocolate cake
for the first time in my life. Did I like that! [Note: Matthew was
healed at age three and a half during an all-night prayer session at
his home with family and friends from his church.]

The first time I stood up alone to tell the story of my healing
was at a nursing home. It was very special for me to tell what God
had done. I've found you can't always share the same way with
everybody. Christians encourage each other in faith that's based
on the Bible. But for someone who hasn't met the Lord yet, it can
be mind-boggling if you plunge into the depths of the Bible. I
know you do have to use the Bible when you tell about Jesus,
because it's His story. The Bible's the best. You take any up-to-
date newspaper and you'll get a report on what has happened, but
only the Bible can say what's going to happen.

Even though everybody needs to hear about Jesus, you just
can't pipe up on your own without checking it out with the Holy
Spirit. If you crash in on somebody at a wrong time for that person, you can be a stumbling block and offend him so he doesn't

want to ever hear. The Holy Spirit has to open the door before you go in. We've found fun ways to present the gospel.

Last year, my friend Ryan and I cut doors into two big refrigerator boxes to do a skit our church called, "Choose you this day." We make up skits and plays with our friends, the Ferris girls. Together, we did a little revision on the book "Don't Hug a Grudge" [by Donna Peregini] to act out at Parkwoods Manor [for seniors]. Our Sunday school asked us to put it on again with the girls for the pre-school and kindergarten. We all had a ball – the little kids, too.

Just doing things for people can help show God's love, too. When all the kids, teens and adults of our CARE group [church house group] put on a free car wash, we handed out tracts about Jesus. One man said, "Kid, why're you doing this?" So I told him Christians like helping 'cause God cares for people, and I told him how he could have God, too.

74 ———

■

MEMORIES THAT BIND

*Being raised in an alcoholic home with fifteen brothers and sisters,
Kathy Calverly has had a sharp learning curve on how to best
mother her four daughters. But her openness about her journey has led to
numerous opportunities to share Jesus.*

Growing up on a First Nations reserve was lonely and shameful. I always felt inferior. I never was encouraged to go out and "be something." Life was motion with no purpose. My pre-teen years led me to addictions with smoking, drinking and drugs. My role models lived that way, so I followed suit. By the time I started questioning that type of life I was married and had two children.

Gradually I began to long for purpose, and one summer during my search, the desire for smoking and drinking was completely taken away. Eager to give my children the privileges my childhood lacked, we enrolled our daughter in a Christian school. One of the school's stipulations was that the parents must attend a church. We decided to go to the church where the school was held. We thought we would go a couple of times and eventually they would not even notice us there and we'd fade away. But shortly after our first Sunday, the pastor came to visit at our home and while he was there he led my husband to the Lord.

I was completely ignorant of what took place but sensitive to what my husband was experiencing. Immediately I noticed a spirit of peace in Brad. Our church visits continued and about a month later the pastor was speaking on Sodom and Gomorrah. I really could identify with that story. I had experienced sexual sins throughout my life and I could identify with how wrong and shameful it felt. That morning I surrendered my life to Christ. I asked for forgiveness; the Lord Jesus Christ came into my life, and things have never been the same.

The path of growing to know Jesus better has been deeply healing to my soul. God continually brings people alongside me who love, teach and encourage me. For example, one day *100 Huntley Street*'s guests were Fred and Florence Littauer. They were sharing their new book *Free Your Mind From Memories That Bind*. During this show I felt anxiety and fear and I knew they were talking about me. In that moment I cried out to God to help me deal with these scary issues.

That was four years ago. I now know that when I first became a believer God did not bring these things to mind because I could not have handled it. When the time was right, like that morning I was stirred by the television, God began the next step to healing.

Through good, loving Christian people who did not expect anything back, I was loved, listened to, encouraged and nurtured to a wholeness that allowed me to learn how to have healthy relationships. God's timing is so perfect. He has shown me that on the road to healing, relationships are number one; first the relationship with God, then others.

I have learned that being vulnerable and humble is not something to be ashamed of, and that we share Christ best when we do so from the lessons of our life. Both in initiating the healing and in His leading since, the Holy Spirit has asked me to leave my comfort zone and to take risks for His kingdom. This has often meant God has led me to go beyond the church walls, back into the First Nations community. Our First Nations people lack natives reaching natives. My heart is with my people. Yes, we are unique, but beautiful and with so much potential.

For the past three years the Lord has led me to start a girls' club on the reserve, which provides an opportunity to be a role model, to build trust, to share Jesus. To see the girls leave at the end of the year with confidence in themselves is a wonderful thing. This has opened the door to speak on native wellness and to leading a Positive Indian Parenting group. This uses a secular curriculum but we open in prayer with these parents to show how much God loves and cares for them and their families. This has opened tremendous doors to witness on the reserve. Progress is slow because the ability to trust people is not there. To change we need quantity personal time to build relationships.

God says we are to be salt of the earth and I hope I am. My calling is to glorify God daily and I love to do my best to please Him. His first command is to love as I have loved you. I have experienced and felt His love and now I want to give it back.

MANIC DEPRESSIVE, BUT EMPOWERED

Sometimes circumstances threaten to prevent us from releasing spiritual gift-edness that God has placed in us. We can overcome that, says denominational leader Danny Gales, who teaches on that subject. He points to his friend Gerry, a fifty-six-year-old overcomer of manic depression.

At the age of nine, Gerry Hay's journey through life took a destructive dive when he was traumatically abused. By age ten he was drinking heavily. A learning disability compounded his social estrangement and Gerry became involved in teenage crime. At twenty-nine and in a jail cell, he committed his life to Christ withthe help of the Salvation Army and Alcoholics Anonymous.

After his release from jail, Gerry worked in the mines of northern Manitoba but when his health caused him to leave that work, he yearned to be a pastor. Eager for education, a stint in Bible college ended in disappointment with Gerry hospitalized for manic depression. Through the discipleship of a friend, he began to understand who he was and how God could use him.

Gerry was about fifty when he took a personality profile test. It showed that he had the spiritual gift of pastoring.

"That's exactly what he had always wanted to do, but because of his condition as a manic depressive he asked himself, 'How can I pastor if I don't have the emotional strength' for the job?" said Danny. "But Gerry is a phenomenal example in how he kept looking toward that gift, and he has found a unique application of it. It has been empowering for him and the cause of Christ.

"Gerry will tell you that all he does is pray, but that is a release of his shepherding heart and in the past two years he can document more than eighty people who have made commitments to Christ since they've been on his prayer list."

Indeed, Gerry's prayer list, which names more than 4,600 people, is anything but typical. Organized in two three-ring binders, Gerry has compiled more than 1,000 names of people he meets in his neighbourhood and daily trips to shopping malls or coffee shops. Living close to a university, many of his contacts are students.

"Gerry has a wonderful way of 'working a room,' " said Danny. "You can just watch him introduce himself and get to know people, and all those contacts will be put into Gerry's book."

Gerry's second binder, a red one, is a collection of what he calls "centres of influence." Culled from denominational head office sources and ministry contacts, it holds names of leaders, ministers and lay people whom Gerry commits to pray for.

"I pray God's will to be done for them, I follow the Lord's prayer for these people and I pray these believers will exercise their gifts for God," said Gerry.

Unable to be employed, his daily discipline includes mornings spent in Bible study and a prayer walk. Afternoons, he spends several hours praying through the names in his prayer binder. Gerry and his wife Betty live simply on her wage as a nanny, their disability pension, and income from boarders. But they give lavishly of their gifts to pray for the salvation of everyone they meet.

■

ENCOUNTER "HIT" LIST

When Gaye Shoemaker found she was on a prayer list from a phone book, she realized God was not as distant as she thought. She believes those who prayed for her are hidden heroes who enabled her to reach God's peace.

My forty-year journey to faith has taken me across the spiritual spectrum. Negativity, fear and legalism characterized my childhood church and I grew to have a great contempt for all Bible-believing, born-again Christians. In my opinion, evangelicals had all committed intellectual suicide. Instead, I turned to liberal churches, and then investigated Judaism, Islam and eastern religious philosophies. Through later involvement with the New Age movement I developed my own unique view of God, but in spite of my newly evolved spirituality and mystical nearness to God I was dissatisfied with my life.

In the fall of 1990 I attended my uncle's funeral at an evangelical church. I was appalled when the pastor began to preach the gospel and a number of people chimed in with "Amen" and "Praise the Lord." I couldn't believe it. These born-again Christians would take advantage of any opportunity to evangelize – even a funeral. I left the church absolutely furious, determined never to enter a church again, and turned my back on God.

That winter was the blackest time I have ever experienced. Life was meaningless. I was miserable, and eventually I went to my doctor for help. As it turned out, my doctor was a Christian, and when she was unable to help me medically she asked, "Gaye, why don't you just lay your burden at the feet of Jesus?" As she tried to share the gospel with me, I became very angry and we ended up in an argument. Finally, she just pointed to the Bible on her desk and said, "Either you believe it, or you don't." I looked her straight in the face and said, "I don't," and stormed out. My depression got worse.

Then, on the long weekend in May, I came home to discover a message on my answering machine from my aunt. I had not seen her since my uncle's funeral at the church two years before, and was really quite surprised to hear from her. I called back and received an invitation to lunch, along with the inevitable invitation to church. Obligingly I went, armed with my usual prejudices and opinions, but to my surprise I enjoyed the service. People welcomed me and the pastor even offered a listening ear if I ever needed to talk. Afterwards, back at my aunt's house, I said, "You know, Aunt Vi, I've been really down these past few months and I enjoyed today. Just what made you call me, anyway?"

"Well, Gaye," she said, "lately I've been feeling the Lord prodding me to call you, so finally I did. You see, I've been praying for you and your family for years but, in the last six months, I've been praying for you every day. Your name is on my *Why Encounter* list."

She had signed up to pray for a list of names from the phone book. I looked at the list and, sure enough, of all the names in the Toronto phone book, she got the page with my name on it. Could this be just a coincidence?

Back at my apartment building, I got into the elevator with two women. One reached into her purse, smiled, and handed me a little book. On the cover was a happy-face with the words, "Smile, Jesus loves you." Inside the front cover was the question, "Are you a Christian?" I knew God was trying to tell me something.

I went to church again the next week, and my aunt marshalled prayer warriors at the church. My name was on a list at their weekly prayer meeting and the ladies' prayer chain. When I later met these people, it brought tears to my eyes to think that people who had never even met me cared enough to pray.

One Sunday in June was baptism day and I was moved by the service and testimonies. When they began to play the hymn "Just As I Am," the pastor invited people to come forward and receive the Lord. I could no longer hold back the tears as I made my way to the front. I tried to pray but couldn't. Something was stopping me. The pastor came and asked if I had ever been involved in the occult. I remembered the Ouija board, the tea leaves and the tarot-card readings, the fortune tellers, the astrology charts and the New Age psychic I had consulted. The pastor explained that such prac-

tices could lead to bondage and demonic oppression. He asked if
I wanted to be free, and to accept Jesus Christ as my Lord and
Saviour.

"Yes," I replied tearfully. As he prayed for me, I had trouble
hearing him at times and I experienced nausea and weakness. God
was fighting for my soul and Satan did not want to let go. Finally,
the pastor said "Cease striving, and know that I am God" (Psalm
46:10). Within a few minutes I was smiling and full of peace.

That was two years, three months and seven days ago. Jesus
said, "I am the way and the truth and the life. No one comes to
the Father except through me" (John 14:6). I believe that with all
my heart, and believing that has changed my life.

■

P RAYING – C ARING – S HARING

*Tom Taylor, a "basically reserved" man, learned early in his Christian
life the importance of building relationships and spending time with
people – whether friends, strangers, university students or street people.
Though he and his wife Shery insist they do not have the gift of
evangelism, their example shows that it is availability and commitment
that count. Shery tells the story.*

From the moment God's Spirit touched his heart at age twenty-
three, Tom Taylor has been a different man. He was not looking
for God, not wanting religion nor seeking an experience, but after
reading his childhood Bible for many hours, he was overwhelmed
with his sin against God and wanted to make it right. All he knew
to do was to kneel down by his bed and cry out for help and sal-

vation. After that his habits and his language changed, and he read the Bible regularly. There had been a great void in his heart that the Holy Spirit had filled.

Very soon, Tom tried to tell people he worked with what had happened to him, and that they needed God too, but he didn't know how to give people the truth plus show love and acceptance. Some mature Christians spent time with Tom, teaching him how to have a relationship with Jesus through prayer and the Word of God. They also helped him to know how to talk to others about Jesus.

It was during this time that I met him – a handsome but quiet guy. We found ourselves thinking, planning and making our life decisions based on how we could help fulfil Christ's Great Commission.

When we were married twenty-seven years ago, we wanted to obey God and do His will. What form this was to take, or what our lives would look like exactly, we didn't know. We have tried to obey God step by step.

During the first two years of our marriage, we gave up some of our evenings and weekends to invite young men from a military air base for sports and food. Later on we moved several times, from Denver to Edmonton, Calgary, Kingston, and finally to Halifax, where we now live.

My basically reserved husband began to spend time with people daily, building relationships and looking for opportunities to discuss the good news of Jesus. Meanwhile, I was starting to raise our children. Often, we would invite people for a meal. It was not difficult except when the baby was fussy and had to be carried everywhere, or the toddler had not napped at her usual time and was crying for attention. Then I would get behind schedule and fret about not being ready. Things would go from bad to worse in my private world of commitment to the Great Commission.

I loved the world for Jesus' sake, but when my comfort level was passed, I didn't like it at all. But we pressed on one step at a time.

The next step was another move, this time to Kingston. There, we made contact with students at Queens University. Tom and a friend stood at the busiest intersection of the campus and began to take religious-interest surveys to see if anyone wanted to use the Bible to discuss life issues. They started meeting with a few guys, and before long before we had a large group of men and women, many of whom received Christ as personal Saviour and Lord because Tom took time for them.

A few years later Tom began to spend lunch hours in a downtown mall. Inviting another Christian friend to join him, he would sit in the busiest area and wait for someone to sit down beside them. Soon they would be in conversation, and before long would find opportunities to talk about Jesus in relation to life needs.

Our four daughters were included as often as possible in conversation or activity that brought people into our home. In the early days, they justifiably could have complained that we hardly ever did anything by ourselves as a family. But most of the time the extra people made life more fun, because there were more people to play with them. As new parents we had prayed for God to make up to our children anything they would miss because of our choices. We did not know even half of the extent of the meaning of that prayer.

One of our most significant steps in following Jesus' Great Commission came when we started going on two-hour prayer walks, praying for our city of Halifax and all the people groups in it. We would ask "the Lord of the Harvest" to send labourers into the harvest of each place that came to our attention.

When you walk around most cities' downtown areas, you cannot miss the people of the streets, so we prayed for labourers for the streets, where Christians ought to be seen loving and caring for people rather than ignoring them or leaving them to social services.

Little by little God drew our hearts to the hurting and helpless. We met others who also had such a heart and were doing something already about the needs or wanted to. God led us to do something ourselves and encourage others. We discovered that we needed to hang out with street people and to be available any time. Tom is especially good at meeting them for coffee to listen, talk and express to them, "I accept you even if you're not all cleaned up and put together."

A side benefit of this has been that our grown up kids are involved too, and it ministers to them and to their friends. Another benefit is the team effort needed in this kind of work. We need many gifts to meet the needs of hurting people, so we team up with other ministries to pray and provide special events.

Tom does not have "the gift of evangelism," but he has been available for God's Spirit to lead him. Many people have seen his sincerity, have felt his interest in them as individuals, and have heard the truth about forgiveness and life in Jesus Christ. Tom does not do this because it is easy or because it is all he can do, but because many years ago God touched his life with His words of love, and it is a good way to be thankful. I'm glad I have been a part of this adventure. I do not have a gift of evangelism either, but God has me as part of the team.

BETWEEN THE LINES

Nancy Ford claims to have 180 children, five of them biological, 175 by correspondence.

At age sixty, my retirement from nursing lay before me like a road I could hardly wait to travel. It seemed to me that this was God's time, and my heart's desire was to do ministry.

You might need to know that I am a pretty typical grandmother – I love to knit, garden, pickle and make jellies and yes, my house is usually clean. My nine grandchildren come and go with their lovely parents, but I was keeping my eyes open for a "made for Nan" ministry opportunity. I took on a week as a camp nurse at a Scripture Union baseball camp at Pickering, Ontario, and I found that the most exciting part of camp was to see children accept Christ. It was also a joy to watch them dig into their cabin time devotionals.

I learned that each summer, more than 10,000 Canadian kids use Scripture Union devotional materials during their stay at camp. It was one of the titbits I gleaned from meeting Marge at camp, the director's wife at Scripture Union. Marge's work was to correspond with some of those children and, through the mail, teach them the joy of having a daily quiet time with Jesus.

But Marge and her husband were heading back to school. She had just resigned her volunteer post and was looking for someone to fill her shoes. By the time we were done talking, my heart was stirred and I said yes immediately.

So for the past two years this is how God has answered my prayer to be in ministry for Him. I spend twenty to thirty hours a week as the Scripture Union Correspondence Club secretary. My wages are not packaged like they used to be. Rather, I now cash in the precious resource the Bible can be to a new Christian. These are pretty special kids I correspond with. We reach them through a quarterly Bible-reading guide Scripture Union sends to about 3,000 children. Of those, only about 175 children say yes, they want more Bible study in their lives. And so we begin a gentle read-as-you-go discipleship with children all across Canada. I even have one girl in the Northwest Territories. I view each of those 175 kids with the same kind of concern I had for own family's spiritual growth, only these kids know me and write to me as "Aunt Nancy."

Perhaps God had me prepared especially for this job because I know from personal experience how important it is to communicate with God through the Bible. For a long time now, I have made it my goal to read the entire Bible through each year. Now I find that habit has not only strengthened my relationship with God, but has increased the knowledge I can pass on to my corre-

spondence children.

My husband has eagerly piggybacked into this ministry. He helps with maintenance at the Scripture Union office and does a lot of work on the newsletter I send out to the children every quarter. Together we pray for these dear children and that I will have the discernment to read between the lines on some of the questions they send me, like the little girl who lived in a home where no one was a Christian; she wrote to ask "How do you know the Bible wasn't written by a normal man?" In my response, I included Scripture Union's book *How We Know The Bible*, which explains the Bible's authenticity. I am still waiting to hear from her.

I try to encourage these children to go to Sunday school and be part of a church in their area. Again, I know from personal experience how important this is. If they show up at your Sunday school, will you give them a hug and tell them it's from Aunt Nancy?

■

TAKING THE RISK

A story is told of an Indian who found an eagle's egg and put it into the nest of a prairie chicken. The eaglet hatched and grew up with the brood of chicks.

All his life the misplaced eagle, thinking he was a prairie chicken, did what chickens did. He scratched in the dirt for seeds and insects. He clucked and cackled. He flew, with a brief thrash of wings and flurry of feathers, no more than a few feet off the ground. After all, that's how prairie chickens fly.

Years passed and the misplaced eagle grew very old. One day, he saw a magnificent bird far above him in the cloudless sky. Hanging with graceful majesty on the powerful wind currents, it soared with scarcely a beat of its strong golden wings.

"What a beautiful bird!" said the misplaced eagle to his neighbour. "What is it?"

"That's an eagle – the chief of the birds," the neighbour clucked. — 89 "But don't give it a second thought. You could never be like him."

So the misplaced eagle never gave it another thought, and died thinking it was a prairie chicken. What a tragedy! Built to soar into the heavens, but conditioned to stay earthbound, he pecked at stray seeds and chased insects. Though designed to be among the most awesome of all birds, instead he believed his neighbour's counsel: "Hey, you're only a prairie chicken. Come on, let's go find some insects."

How easy it is to take everything for granted. Even though God may have intended for you and I to soar like eagles, we may find ourselves living like prairie chickens. To fully become all He has planned for us requires a major step of faith. Reading through the Old Testament, it becomes obvious that many major accomplishments began when God's people recognized:

1) it was impossible by natural means;

2) the need for implicit trust in God;

3) their absolute dependence on God's miracle-working power.

The stories in this chapter show that there is no easy "scratch and win" approach that guarantees a winning outcome. Although God never changes, He is full of surprises when it comes to accomplishing His work. All He asks is that we move beyond our comfort zones by faith.

– dm

Dear friends, do you think you'll get anywhere in this if you learn all the right words but never do anything? Does merely talking about faith indicate that a person really has it? For instance, you come upon an old friend dressed in rags and half-starved and say, "Good morning, friend! Be clothed in Christ! Be filled with the Holy Spirit!" and walk off without providing so much as a coat or a cup of soup – where does that get you? Isn't it obvious that God-talk without God-acts is outrageous nonsense?

James 2:14-17 (TM)

WORKING THE STREETS

Setting out to love Winnipeg's street people, Larry and Loretta Becker unwittingly set up their first outreach in the city's red-light district. It was not a comfort zone for them, but it has developed into a fruitful ministry.

With a sign declaring "Love Lives Here," a mobile van to serve coffee, and a heart for the people of the streets, Larry and Loretta Becker launched a ministry in one of the roughest parts of Winnipeg a decade ago. It was not until people began commenting on the sign that the couple realized the significance of their location.

"We didn't know it was a prostitution area," said Loretta.

They did know they were drawn to the streets where the unloved and the unlovely make their home, although neither of them felt comfortable about being in the midst of street life.

"It was a real longing inside us to work on the streets," Loretta recalled, "like an inner urging of the Holy Spirit."

Larry, a sign painter, and Loretta, a travel agent, began sharing their vision with Christian friends. With the help of friends Bruce and Sandra Day, they launched the ministry that has since made hundreds of contacts and seen many people come to the Lord. Today Love Lives Here has one full-time worker and about two dozen volunteers who go to the streets once or twice a week or work behind the scenes.

That first night a hooker asked the Beckers to move their van because it was blocking her business. Later that night she came in for a cup of coffee and began talking. It turned out she had been involved in music ministry herself in the past. The last place she expected Christians to turn up was on the corner where she worked.

"We ended up having a lot of contact with her," says Larry. The woman eventually left the street.

Because the neighbourhood around Main Street and just north of downtown is very transient, the Beckers often lose track of people they have met. Sometimes they show up two or three years later, after being in prison or moving away, and are surprised that the ministry centre – now a permanent trailer on Martha and Henry – is still there.

"We know that when God starts a work in someone, He'll bring it to completion," Larry reasons.

There are other times when a persistent, caring relationship bears visible fruit. Anna, for example, started working the streets when she was about twelve. Originally from Czechoslovakia, she had been abused, and turned to prostitution for her livelihood. The Beckers befriended her and talked to her whenever they met.

Then they went to Regina to start a similar ministry with volunteers there. And there was Anna, on the streets.

"You're following me," she accused them. Like many prostitutes, Anna would move from one city to another and back again, looking for business. When she returned to Winnipeg the contact was maintained.

"One time she came to the trailer and said her pimp had dragged her through the mall by her hair," said Larry. Children's Aid had custody of her daughter and Anna was pregnant with another child.

Anna eventually became a Christian, was freed from a cocaine addiction, got her daughter back and in August of 1994 married the full-time worker at Love Lives Here. When the Beckers make presentations about the ministry at churches, Anna sometimes gives her testimony.

About the same time Anna began visiting the trailer, a young man named Sean started dropping in.

"He looked like your typical nice little boy, but he wasn't," said Larry. It turned out he was heavily into drug dealing and used to rob banks. But one night he walked into the trailer and said, "I want to do it tonight. I want to make a commitment tonight." Sean made a complete turnaround in his life, and is now on staff at a Winnipeg church.

There are heartaches, too. Loretta can name five people who have died violent deaths. All five knew the Lord when they died. One woman who was off the street for about eight years, married and had a child, recently returned to street life. Things like that can be discouraging. Sometimes it is only by the grace of God that the ministry keeps going.

Remaining committed to people and to the ministry is important. "It seems like a lot of the people are very open to the gospel," Larry said. "They see that you're sincere, not just there to hand out a few tracts."

Though there are sacrifices, the couple would rather spend their free time with people nobody else wants anything to do with.

"I see a life change as really exciting; and it's satisfying," Larry summed it up. "I don't think you're going to find it sitting in a church pew.

"A lot of people don't have hope on the street," he pointed out. "That's why we operate Love Lives Here. It gives them hope, and that hope is in Jesus Christ.

■

SENIOR GOES TO PRISON

The name Lillian Marshall is a "household word" in New Brunswick prisons, according to a former inmate she befriended who is now in full-time prison ministry himself. It all started with hearing a hymn one night in church.

A few months after her husband died suddenly in 1973, Lillian Marshall heard the words of a hymn in church in a way she had never heard them before: "I'll go where you want me to go, dear

Lord; I'll do what you want me to do." She was sixty years old, and this was her first Sunday back to church in Moncton, New Brunswick after her husband had died in her arms of a heart attack.

"That night when they sang that hymn, it seemed I couldn't get clear of it." Shortly after that her pastor's wife called her to ask if Lillian would host the mother of an inmate. She had come from Alberta and had nowhere to stay. She stayed with Lillian for a couple of weeks.

"She asked her son if I could visit him," Lillian recalled. "He said, 'I don't want any old lady to visit me.'

"She said, 'She has the years, but she's like a young person.' "

The son gave in. "We had a lovely visit. . . . We became very, very good friends."

That first visit turned into many more, and soon other inmates were requesting visits from Lillian Marshall. When the first young man was transferred from Dorchester to Prince Albert, Saskatchewan, Lillian took vacation time to visit him there. And when he was transferred to Millhaven, near Kingston, Ontario, she boarded a train once a month to see him there.

For eight years Lillian organized her weekends around prison visits: Saturday mornings were for Dorchester (maximum security); Saturday afternoons were spent at the farm camp (minimum); and Sunday afternoons were at Spring Hill (medium).

"They were all wanting me to visit them," she explained. If prisoners' parents came from out of town, Lillian gave them a place to stay and a car to drive to and from the prison.

It did not matter that she had little in common with most of the men she met in jail.

"They just wanted to know what I had done, and where I had been," she said. "I'd ask them, 'What did you used to do?' and just try to encourage them."

She also encouraged them to attend chapel services, and talked to them about the Lord. Some of them were very receptive. Others "didn't want to hear it at all."

One fellow who had a keen interest in spiritual things was Ernie LeBlanc, whom she met in 1976. Ernie, now a chaplain at county jails, accepted the Lord shortly after he went to prison. He describes his old friend as "a great woman of God – very compassionate, very understanding, very helpful.

"We don't see God, but we see people," he pointed out. "God is seen through her." When Ernie got out of jail and was having a hard time financially she was there to help him. "She was the first to support me when I stepped out in the ministry," Ernie said. "She always puts others before herself."

Not every inmate she made friends with was as trustworthy as Ernie. She invited one fellow who "seemed to have a great potential" to come live with her after his release. She was working in the insurance business and he encouraged her to start her own business. She did, and took him on as a partner. He later stole money from her.

"He did take me for a ride and left me to walk home," she admitted, adding, "That's his problem, not mine."

Betrayals such as that one did not stop her. "I was always hoping that I could do something even though they might let me down," she said.

"Even in the hurts she still loved," said Ernie. "Through physical and mental stress, she still loved the individual no matter what."

Although Lillian stopped her prison visits in 1981 (and retired from the insurance business in 1993 at age eighty), she still keeps in touch with some of her friends from prison. The first man she visited phones or writes about once a year. Through the years

Lillian Marshall's family has been supportive of her ministry.

"At first they were absolutely horrified," she said. "But then when they began to see what I was doing and why I was doing it, they were in complete co-operation."

A deep sense of compassion motivated Lillian to become involved in people's lives despite the risks.

"I just had a desire that I loved to help someone," she said simply.

And, looking back, "I don't regret any of it."

■

F O O D :   A   W A Y   T O   T H E   H E A R T

Would your church let you use their dishes at home? In North Vancouver, a chapel found that co-operation of that kind helped spawn a unique ministry for evangelism.

When Les's wife dragged him to the Sunday school picnic, the pastor was one of the people she introduced him to.

"The first thing he said to me was, 'I'll never come to church,' " recalled Pastor Greg Webster (names in this story are not real), who gingerly steered the conversation to a less threatening ground. An avid tennis player, Greg discovered that Les also played the game, and was looking for a partner. Soon the two were meeting for early morning games twice a week.

Someone else at that church had a very different hobby. Alison Tyler loved to cook. She and her husband Bruce became intrigued with the idea of hosting dinner parties that would present the message of Christianity. The Tylers moved all the furniture out of the living and dining room area of their townhouse, and set up for a dinner they hoped twenty people would attend.

They learned their strategy from an uncle who hosted something similar:

– serve an appetizer and play an icebreaker;

– enjoy a great meal together;

– have an invited speaker share the gospel in a relevant and seeker-friendly manner;

– close with a dessert buffet.

Alison and Bruce bought stationary and printed up invitations on a home computer. These they personally presented to pre-Christian friends and acquaintances. That first venture developed into a habit, and in the past eight years Alison and Bruce's dinner parties have evolved into an evangelism outreach of the supportive congregation of which they are members.

They host such gatherings three times a year, and now own a home which can accommodate forty people for dinner. A friend from church comes to help the Tylers move all the furniture into their son's bedroom and carry in dishes and four round tables from the church. The dinners cost about ten dollars per guest to host, and the Tylers were thrilled when in year five the church began covering a third of their costs.

"We pay for this out of savings, but we're just like a normal family and hardly ever have savings, so there are times the dinners come out of our tithe," explained Alison. "I cook all the food ahead of time; it's just something simple – ham and scalloped potatoes, or chicken in mushroom sauce. I find that people love having food that tastes like a mother cooked it."

For all eight years of the hosting, her friend Janice has worked in the kitchen for those evenings and enlisted four others from church to be servers. The Tylers relax and enjoy the meal with their guests, including friends from church who have also invited pre-Christian friends.

They never pray before these meals because they know many in the room are already well outside their comfort zones. Prayer is left to the speaker, who sensitively hands out comment cards and if suitable, literature on Christianity as he or she speaks.

When Alison and Bruce invited professional athlete Rick Ryan as a dinner speaker, Pastor Greg decided his tennis partner Les would be ready to hear the gospel. It had been more than two years since the church picnic and Les's last encounter with a church-sponsored event.

"Les is a sports nut in every area so he came to hear Rick and was on the edge of his seat," explained Greg. That dinner was the start for Les. He soon made a commitment to Christ.

At two recent church baptisms, believers credited the starting point of their walk with Christ to an encounter in the Tyler home. Bruce and Alison watch the faces of their guests; if they see emotion or sense conviction, they will later phone them. By following the Holy Spirit's prompting, the Tylers have had many opportunities to introduce someone to a home Bible study or Sunday morning service.

The frequency of these parties has given all of the church a focus to keep nurturing friendships outside the church.

"The Tylers' work dovetailed so nicely into a need our church had," explained Greg. "We knew our church was filled with nice people, but a survey exposed the weakness in that we knew only Christian people." The dinner parties have been an outcome of that realization that they needed to get to know more non-Christians.

Now the church hopes to host a purely social function at least twice a year to offer its members a non-religious context in which to foster secular friendships. The church also sponsors a year-round "Operation Andrew" prayer ministry in which members write down the names of four non-Christian friends for whom they are praying. The church elders receive a copy of each list and add their prayers.

"I think prayer is the most important thing in all of this," said Alison. Aside from her daily time with God, she meets with a friend every Wednesday morning at 6:30 a.m. for an hour of prayer.

"To both Bruce and me, prayer is the most important thing in this venture."

■

THE INK TELLS THE STORY — 99

Does tract ministry still work? Jerry Saylor says "Yes" and suits action to his words.

Despite the risk of ridicule, Jerry Saylor has handed out hundreds of thousands of tracts in the past twenty-five years – from Sydney, Nova Scotia to Sydney, Australia.

"There's been a real change over the years," said Jerry, reviewing his long experience with tract distribution. "People are more polite now. Nobody tells me to 'f--- off' any more, and almost nobody throws them on the ground. People say 'thank you' and put them in their pockets. People's hearts have grown softer; they're more hungry."

Occasionally a tract can lead to conversation and even conversion right on the street, he said, but more often people put it in a pocket or purse.

Since moving to Calgary in 1991 Jerry has made it a habit to spend Wednesday mornings walking the streets handing out tracts, talking to people and visiting with them in coffee shops. When people ask him why he gives out tracts, he explains that "God put it in my heart to do this. I love talking to people about Jesus and the change He makes in your life when you accept Him."

For the past two years Jerry has been working as a church custodian, the latest in a long series of time-flexible jobs that enable him to devote large blocks of time to tract distribution. Since taking this job in 1992, he has been able to make tract-distribution trips with his wife Helen to Yellowknife, Northwest Territories and to Sydney, Australia where he took 50,000 tracts, all of which Jerry and Helen folded by hand.

Even after twenty-five years of distributing tracts, Jerry is still amazed that God chose him for the job.

"At first I was very shy and afraid, and I would stumble over words. I'm not a very good speaker – not eloquent or articulate."

Jerry first launched into tract ministry in 1969 in Sydney, Nova Scotia. He was a shy young man who had just moved from his family home town to begin work at a K-Mart department store. His new pastor encouraged him to distribute tracts and, much to Jerry's surprise, his boss at work also thought the idea was a good one. Jerry went from distributing a few hundred in Sydney that first day to making regular trips to nearby cities such as Halifax. By the time he left Nova Scotia thirteen years later, he had placed a standing order of 6,000 tracts per month from his supplier. Since then, he has never looked back. In cities across Canada he has given the gospel to anyone he meets on the street. One memorable place for him is Vancouver, where he moved in 1986 to minister to visitors to Expo. There he lived in a dingy hotel and spent time praying, fasting and distributing tracts to people in the city as tract distribution was not permitted on the Expo grounds.

"There was a drug pusher in the hotel, and I prayed for him for over a year," said Jerry. "He actually accepted Jesus and quit dealing drugs. It turned out his parents had been enrolled in the Salvation Army so that's where he went."

As Jerry speaks of his life's itinerary, he speaks of God sending him to places. God gives him ideas, and Jerry follows the instructions as best he can. He spends time in prayer and devotion every morning and is convinced that prayer is where he receives his power. Nowadays Jerry is praying about the possibility of he and his wife becoming involved in some kind of full-time team ministry.

"Whenever Jerry gives someone a tract," said Helen, "he says, 'Jesus loves you.' There are a lot of people out there who are down, who need to hear that. A word like that, getting and reading a tract – those things are never wasted on a person."

■

THE INVISIBLE CHURCH

For David Morehouse and his congregation, getting serious about the great commission meant buying a Sunday school bus even though only two children showed up – and then finding ways to fill the bus.

As a recent seminary graduate, David Morehouse found himself on the steps of a small country church on the outskirts of Moncton, New Brunswick. He faced a century-old church which described itself as "in crisis." The congregation had dwindled to about 50 with a Sunday school of two children.

There are basically three types of churches, a seminary professor had warned David Morehouse as he contemplated a career in pastoring. There are comfortable churches with no desire for change: don't go there. There are a minority of churches where revival is actually happening: if you are so fortunate as to be called there, go. Then, there are churches in crisis: the ones that are dying or stagnating. Choose those churches for ministry, the professor had advised.

During David's interview with the pulpit committee, one member predicted the church would be closed within three years. David left the session knowing in his heart God was calling him to this church.

Since then, David and his congregation have sought to relearn what they call "the melody of mission." They have struggled, debated, tested one another's levels of faith and patience, and they have rejoiced.

102 ——

"We had become a little country church that had failed to incorporate the community," explained David. "Our little white church had become invisible to the community." He set out to change that by striving to reawaken his congregation to the Great Commission. At the beginning of every meeting, he would pose the question: "What are we here for?" The answer he was always looking for, and the one congregation members soon learned to echo to him, was simple, yet strong: "Making disciples."

Despite the fact that there were very few children – sometimes none – in the church, David began telling a weekly children's story and including a children's hymn in the service.

"I wanted to prepare for the day when a family with children came to the church; they would know we had a desire to minister to them."

As new, young families began to come, the congregation agreed to turn the women's parlour into a nursery. Members were pressed to put faith into action, and the majority responded to the ensuing challenges positively.

"I constantly pushed what I call an outreach posture for our congregation," said David. "We had to get serious about the great commission of love, the great commission of making disciples." Tangibly, that meant that if a Sunday school class had an outing, it was not considered a success unless there had been new people there. It meant that getting children out to Sunday school necessitated the purchase of a bus, even though the fifty-seat bus had only two children on it for the first few months. Then the posture of mission meant finding ways to fill the bus with children.

As an evangelistic effort, the membership decided to have a "Kiss the Pig" challenge.

"We had a goal to get fifty people on the bus for Sunday school," explained David. "If we met this goal, the bus driver promised he would kiss a pig." Word of the challenge spread throughout the community, and on the final Sunday, not only were there fifty kids on the bus, but the church was full.

Another significant growth initiative developed out of Friday morning breakfasts for men. What began with four has grown to a ministry including more than ninety men.

"We started to reach men for Christ and we discovered something – if you reached a guy for Christ, the next week his whole family would be in church," said David. Men on the fringe of church activities began attending. Non-Christian men in the community came. "We've seen a spiritual vitality appearing in more men's lives. Now in addition to the breakfast, there are two men's Bible studies."

As pews began to fill up, the church began to intentionally train members to be friendlier.

"We have a simple rule of thumb: a new person should have his

—— 103

or her hand shaken by five to seven individuals," said David.

The congregation also realized that to have a posture of mission the church had to change physically. As a new building went up the congregation realized again the price of persevering through the long haul. Now, with eight years passed since the pulpit committee feared that closure was imminent, the tiny congregation has grown to more than 220.

"Even though evangelism scares people, they really do want to work through this issue of the Great Commission. They want to see people come, to see lives changed," said David. And in the midst of it, a church has changed as well. It now has one of the largest sanctuaries in the region, representing a growth that seems incongruent to the field-and-farmhouse landscape around it. Most of the members who have joined in the past eight years were either unchurched or people who had left church disillusioned.

The new challenge for David and his congregation will be to continue the process of making disciples – to work at remembering the melody of mission.

■

HOT STUFF IN THE ARCTIC

As a housing administrator for an Inuit community above the Arctic Circle, Billy Arnaquq located what he believed was the best housing in the world for resisting cold weather. With that job finished, he now concentrates on warming hearts for the gospel of Christ.

Broughton Island, Northwest Territories is a rocky island, barren of trees, surrounded by mountains and pristine waters that are ice-filled year round. Located a few hundred miles north of

Frobisher Bay just across from Greenland on the west side of
Baffin Island, its unique beauty is home to Canada's Auyuittuq
National Park. A handful of tourists from around the world travel
here for an exposure to winter temperatures that hover at minus
forty degrees and where, on the best of summer days, it may
reach fifteen degrees.

"But it's getting hotter here!" quipped Billy Arnaquq. He is
talking about revival that he believes is starting to move through
the north. Billy is well qualified to know the spiritual climate of
his people. Aside from his job as assistant manager to the community of 400, he pastors a church he helped establish, and tours
several northern hamlets as a speaker and evangelist.

"I just came back from teaching and preaching at our first
youth conference in Kangirsujjuaa, Quebec for one week and held
the first water baptism ever in Kujjuaq, in Northern Quebec, on
the way back," explained Billy, aged thirty-five. Patiently he helps
the curious understand how evangelism in the north has become
so important to him.

"The spiritual need up here is exactly the same as down south –
exactly," said Billy. "The hearts are the same."

A Christian since 1980, Billy committed his life to Christ during a fellowship meeting in a house at Broughton Island.

"I played the guitar for them and that night the Spirit of God
convicted me and I was born again," said Billy. Billy soon felt a
growing call from God on his life and spent two years at National
Native Bible College to equip his growing faith.

"Since I came to the Lord I have so much compassion for my people it just burns in me to bring Jesus to them," said Billy. "At first my
flesh didn't want to share Jesus, but I obeyed God. Once you start
responding to God and to the need of the people, God gives you
the energy and the drive. Now I am eager in my flesh and my spirit."

So eager that he is praying about quitting his job and going into ministry full time. The church he helped plant has grown to twenty attendees and is ready to sponsor this thirty-five-year-old single dynamo for Jesus into full-time itinerant preaching.

"They are so giving, so generous with sharing for the sake of the gospel," said Billy. The typical family lives on $20,000 a year and lives simply, as Billy estimates that food costs are triple those of the south. The price of a dozen eggs is four dollars, a head of lettuce about the same.

"The people rely on fish, seal, whale and caribou meat. It's cheaper and it's fresher," said Billy.

He mourns the difficult cultural transition his people are undergoing, saying the switch from traditional to modern living happened so fast his people went into shock.

"The thing I like to teach on most is vision, giving my people a vision and hope for the future," said Billy. "You really see the desperation on the young people's faces and it just breaks your heart."

He recalls the story of a youth meeting he spoke at in Arctic Bay. The crowd of forty was an exceptional turnout and many young people came forward to accept Christ that night. But one teenager sat sullenly with his head down and remained motionless.

"I went down and sat beside him; I tried to hold him with my arm around him and he was just limp. He was in total darkness, total despair," said Billy. "After about half an hour he finally opened up a bit, but that experience really spoke to me. It just tore my heart and that night I realized I have to reach these people; there are just too many that are lost."

Since Billy's conversion, his family has been affected by his love for the Lord. All but one of the seven members have made a commitment to the Lord. Most were influenced by various presentations of Billy's ministry.

"We get nine satellite channels up here, we get the same stuff you do in the south and one day my brother saw me speaking on *100 Huntley Street* during native week. He told me he was really touched by my testimony and told me he knew he will have to get saved someday," explained Billy. "About a month later I spoke at an unfinished pool hall in Pangnirtang and he got saved the night before and we made him our guitar player the following night."

Billy is praying that the church he pastors will be equipped with a full-time youth pastor and resources for a growing music ministry. He says music is one of the most powerful tools to reach his people.

But prayer, says Billy, is the key resource. He believes crusade evangelism works well in the north because it is heavily bathed in prayer.

"We need your prayers," said Billy. "We really need your prayers."

CULTIVATING
CREDIBILITY

One pastor was recently heard to say, "I'm no longer pushing my people to share their faith. Rather, I'm encouraging them to develop quality friendships. In the context of a friendship, people soon want to know what makes the difference in our lives. People must see it to believe it."

We would probably be surprised if we took time to identify and count the number of people we have opportunity to encounter weekly outside of the walls of the church. Whether in the workplace, neighbourhood or shopping centre, we have regular contact with dozens of acquaintances and friends. In each case, we have an opportunity to bring an influence for Christ to bear on another person's life. Consider the following two examples.

After I spoke at a morning worship service a young lawyer approached me, affirming my challenge to prayerfully consider the spheres of influence within our reach.

"I'd never thought of striking up a conversation with the gas station attendant where I regularly buy my gas," he said. "But this week I did. I asked the man what he was doing on the weekend. He said he'd likely party up north of the city. He said the city was boring on weekends. I asked if he'd ever thought about going to church for a change. He said no but that he probably should."

The lawyer offered to take him as his guest any time the attendant wanted to go. Who knows where this will lead as the Spirit of God works in this man's life?

Another Christian, employed in middle management, told how he tried to stand for his biblical values by not lying for his boss. He even took some heat for not being willing to cover for his boss through telling "white" lies. One day, however, he was called into his boss's office. With the door shut, the boss entrusted this believer with a very large sum of money, saying he was the only person he could trust. That kind of credibility speaks loudly.

Each of the following stories points to people who are using everyday encounters to influence others with the credibility of their own lives. As we talk with people whose paths we cross, opportunities will emerge to demonstrate and eventually explain God's love. Your credibility with those you influence can provide a natural open door to share your faith.

– dm

Go into the world uncorrupted, a breath of fresh air in this squalid and polluted society. Provide people with a glimpse of good living and of the living God. Carry the light-giving Message into the night so I'll have good cause to be proud of you on the day that Christ returns. You'll be living proof that I didn't go to all this work for nothing.

Philippians 2:15-16 (TM)

A COMMUNITY
OF 28 NATIONALITIES

When it comes to the subject of community involvement, Arc Da Silva
believes Christians should be there, building bridges and modelling action.

After watching the Bloor-Dufferin area of Toronto decline with
an increase of drug dealing and robberies, Arc Da Silva decided
that his own involvement in the community was a key to making it
a safer place for the almost thirty nationalities that inhabit it.

"As part of my church ministry, I'm committed to five hours of
community involvement each week," said thirty-two-year-old Arc,
a full-time associate pastor since 1987. "But I also live in this area,
and I got involved in the community as a resident responding to
an issue. I realized that many of the churches weren't participating and that the community didn't know who we were."

For the young pastor, that realization meant a personal call to
action on his part.

Arc had moved to the multicultural Bloor-Dufferin area of
Toronto, which today boasts about twenty-eight nationalities, with
his parents from Mombasa, Kenya in 1974. Through the years he
watched as the area declined, and drug dealers began roaming the
streets. By the mid-1980s, robberies and break-ins were common,
and needles and condoms were found in backyards.

"The biggest problem in this community is that it has been a
well known drug area," said Arc.

In 1989, the drug problem reached crisis stage and a public
meeting of residents, government officials and politicians was
held at a local high school. Concerned about his neighbourhood,
Arc attended this meeting and also those of the newly formed
Bloor-Lansdowne Committee Against Drugs. For a year, he listened and observed as local leaders sought answers.

"Most of the time, they weren't looking to the church for those
answers," said Arc. "They felt that we had nothing to say."

"In fact, at one point a police command officer told the group, 'Before, I would have said go to the church for help. But I've seen that they don't do anything.'

"I felt that I needed to make a personal commitment to build bridges with them. My peers are the police, and as Christians we need to be modelling what they should be doing. I think involvement is a must. If we want to connect with the neighbourhood, we need to get involved in a positive way. Too often people think of churches as speaking up only on the negative issues."

Finally, Arc decided to roll up his sleeves and get involved. Because of his efforts, he was named chairperson of the Bloor-Lansdowne Committee Against Drugs two years ago. Since then the group has dealt with concerns about the area's economic development, personal and business safety, and social and recreational needs. In the process, several businesses serving as drug havens were closed down.

Now, says Arc, the committee is employing an even more positive approach by identifying potential businesses and attracting them to the area. Storefronts that were once empty are now beginning to fill again. Also, the committee has been offered a grant to establish an economic development plan with several nearby neighbourhoods.

"Community involvement is not a priority for everyone, but it has made some connections for me," said Arc, noting that his willingness to become involved in community work has lent credibility to his job title. "It has provided me with friends in government, and that makes a difference when it comes to sharing the gospel. It has opened a lot of doors.

"It was tempting to invite my contacts to church at first, but I didn't do that for a long time because I didn't want them to think that I was involved just for that reason. Now it's natural because they know and trust me. It's a very slow process, but that's what building bridges is all about."

The police recently asked Arc to talk to people in the community when an officer was shot in the neighbourhood and the police needed information about the suspect. The director of the local community centre asked Arc to counsel a Japanese man who was dying from liver cancer; the man accepted Christ in his hospital room.

Arc says his involvement has been good for his church, which is now reaching into the neighbourhood more through activities such as an annual fall fair. Although the church has long been active in reaching adults and youth, Arc's work has brought increased name recognition. Also, his church and others are beginning to connect with each other to be a more united force in the community.

"The key is for individuals and churches to be sensitive," explained Arc, who was presented the Westender of the Year award in 1993 for his community service. "Doors are opening and we must be ready. It's a matter of being faithful and discerning God's dream for the city's neighbourhoods."

— 115

■

CORPORATE CONNECTIONS

Twice a week, a handful of Bell Telephone employees in Montreal hook up a dedicated line between head office and their heavenly Father. For Gilles Dextraze those sessions have been a vital tool in learning how to be an effective witness in his workplace.

In 1980, newly married and newly employed at Bell Canada, I was born again spiritually. Right from the start my heart was ready to share the good news with everyone the Lord put along my way. But it has taken me some time to learn how to do that.

In 1984 I heard about someone leading Bible studies during lunch and I began to pray that I would be transferred to that office. A year later, God answered my prayer. For a whole year, however, I battled with the temptation of staying at my desk through lunch to continue working on certain projects. It was an act of will to put down my work and go to the noon-hour study. This is a common difficulty for those of us in management. But after that first year I made a commitment to be faithful to my Bible study group. I believe God has honoured this commitment by bringing me success in my job. Those of us who attend these studies have never received any criticism for our involvement and Bell has always freely made available the rooms we need for the study.

Eventually this core of Christians developed a twice-a-week format. Tuesdays was for us and the Thursday study was designed for "seekers." I ardently desired to invite some of my colleagues to come with me and on Tuesdays we in the group would pray for these colleagues.

Eventually, two came, and after four years of study and prayer one of those friends made a decision to follow Jesus of Nazareth.

Later, I learned that the brother of a friend in my church worked in my office tower and that he was interested in spiritual things. I prayed for him, then invited him to a lunch given by the Christian Business Men's Committee. After he heard the speaker's testimony of his faith in Christ, we began a study together and now he regularly attends the Thursday study. Last spring, he prayed and made the decision to follow Jesus.

There are other examples. As a Christian in the workplace, I feel like a pastor in a church. God continues to place people in my path to minister to, to lead them to Jesus. In building bridges of friendship, I can share the good news of the gospel with them. Sometimes it takes a lot of time, sometimes less, but these bridges cannot be destroyed just because certain ones are not ready to follow Jesus.

Since these are colleagues I work with every day, I feel I should make friendly contact and establish a certain level of rapport before I invite a person to the seekers' study. Out of the fifty or sixty colleagues in my department, I have this rapport with perhaps six to eight. I have learned to persevere in prayer for each of them.

One of the difficulties is maintaining an easygoing rapport with those who attended for a while but then dropped out of the study. When our paths cross, or especially if it is someone I work with on a regular basis, they are ill at ease with me after they stop attending. I have learned to just keep praying for those people, to be friendly and try to let them know that no one has turned his back on them and that the door is always open if they should decide to return. This is so important and delicate with people we work with every day.

One other lesson I have learned from being a witness at work is in regard to career decisions. Now, when I face a possible change in responsibility or a transfer to a different branch, I ask myself; will this advance His kingdom in my workplace or will it draw me further away from God and His work for me? Currently I am an administrative director, managing the budget for my district and acting as a training agent for employees who change positions. When I took this job last year, I prayed it through with a Christian colleague, the one who started the studies here. Now, he has accepted a transfer to another building in the city and we both feel this is God's way of planting His work in that building.

THE WHY CLUB

This September as a new crop of grade eight students melted into
their environment at David Thompson Secondary School in Vancouver,
Ralph Bagshaw smiled about the one technique that has not changed
in education. "You can't outlaw love," explained Bagshaw. "You can't
claim it's biased or politically incorrect or that it doesn't fit in our
multicultural world – love can't be legalized out of existence."

During thirty-five years of teaching and counselling in the
public school system Ralph Bagshaw has mentored dozens of
young people into a relationship in Jesus. He believes that over the
years students' needs have increased, but he is convinced the
answers are the same.

"If they haven't got parents who will give them a morality, I
teach them mine," said Ralph. In or out of the classroom, in club
situations, the staff room, in parents' homes or participating at
students' funerals or weddings, Ralph has found his Christianity
welcomed.

His career-long habit has been to begin his day with God at
6 a.m., when he spends an hour reading his Bible and praying
for courage, boldness and the fruits of the Spirit to indwell
him.

In the 1960s, Ralph encountered rebellious youth who felt
strongly – and often wrongly – about rights, responsibilities and
powers.

"What an opportunity to introduce Jesus Christ as the one who
can make a radical and significant difference in an individual,"
said Ralph.

Just beginning his tenure, he taught his friend Wally to play
rugby, and together the pair set up a noon-hour club where they
taught boys to play the sport hard and fast.

"One day after practice, I said something like, 'You guys are great; you're playing competitively but there's a big area of your life that's kind of blank and I want to talk to you about that one of these days. We're going to start up a club to talk about that.' "

The first meeting was full of tension and uncertainty, Ralph recalled, but fifteen grade ten kids crowded into his front room. They sang some rugby songs accompanied on a little organ and then, bridging over, he taught them "Joshua Fit the Battle of Jericho." The guys loved it and it became a theme song. The kids listened intently to a short talk about God. That club grew to become the largest school club in the school's history.

"And to think it all started by befriending a few guys on the rugby field," Ralph reminisced.

Grant Smith was one of the first kids in the club. After four years of being in Ralph's shadow, Grant committed his life to — 119 Christ. He went on to be a staff member with Inter-Varsity Christian Fellowship in British Columbia, and is now a school administrator in Valleyview, Alberta.

"Ralph was not flashy, not flamboyant; his character ran a lot deeper and he was accepting and available to any and all the students," Grant recalled. "He used everything for a discipleship situation and today we're trying to shape our youth group here much like what Ralph did on those Wednesday nights."

The rugby club success was repeated when Ralph moved on to a tough, inner-city school. In his latest posting, he has created a club called the WHY Club, where students are welcome to come with their questions.

"We have ten to eighteen kids coming every week, and they usually come with a question out of the news media – something about democracy or why does God allow a particular disaster. You can always answer these issues biblically," said Ralph.

Grant, who has been Ralph's friend for some thirty years now, says Ralph has had occasion to ask "why" as well.

"He's taken many risks for kids, really been there for them," said Grant. For instance, there was the time he organized a canoe trip and three of the boys broke expedition rules. They took a canoe where they shouldn't have and were drowned when a sudden storm capsized their vessel.

"After our initial grief counselling, it seemed appropriate to start a Bible study, as kids were asking, 'If God is God, why does He allow this?' " said Ralph. "That was in spring of 1993. Two of those kids have become Christians now and we still have the group coming by."

The staff room seems happy to peg Ralph as the resident expert on Christianity. Social Studies teachers lean on him for portions of their Western Civilization lectures. Invited to teach the happenings of the Reformation, he prefaces his comments with three leading questions:

"How do you define 'Christian'? What have been the most significant contributions of Christianity to our civilization? If you were to name the most distinctive contribution of Christianity to us, what would it be?"

The openness with which he shares means that Ralph and his wife Marilyn find about forty kids using the open-door policy of their home. Many of them have entered into a mentoring relationship with the Bagshaws.

Their upcoming retirement brings a smile to their faces – they are convinced it will be a golden opportunity to maximize their zeal for evangelism.

■

Teaching 45,000 Children

Your tax dollars may fund public education but whose values will be instrumental in teaching Canada's children? Curriculum developer Joyce MacMartin decided she knew a good response for that quandary, and en route found a method to share the gospel at work.

My workplace is a daunting setting where you tip-toe gingerly amid political correctness, minority lobby groups and policies and programs that often are weighed according to the benefit or damage they will exert on the possibility of re-election. Life has become increasingly complex with legislation and policy-makers contending with issues that years ago would not have been considered within the scope of government.

Within this milieu, I was handed an assignment to co-ordinate and write the family life education unit for some 45,000 public school children.

It is important to me to bring a Christian witness and mindset to my job. But within a pluralistic, secular public school system where every provincial curriculum document must conform to guidelines that prevent sexism, racism and intolerance, and where emphasis of one religion is not permitted, how does a "Christian" curriculum developer work?

As I thought of the task before me, I was besieged with memories of my own family life. I grew up in a loving, Christian family in a rural setting where we lived in an extended family with my grandparents. As evangelical Christians, my family was a rarity in our district. My grandparents instituted a Sunday afternoon service at our home. In the large parlour, my brother and I would take turns playing the piano for hymn singing. I remember the exuberant joy and carefree atmosphere that prevailed, and particularly the sincerity of the prayers. Years later as I studied English at university, I would reflect on my grandfathers' prayers. To think that a person with very limited schooling could be eloquent as he talked to God amazed me.

Jesus was Lord of our family, and I recall my parents' and grandparents' expressed, unconditional love and support for all the family members. I thought all families had this sense of harmony and peace. I knew nothing of the heartache that I would later learn is prevalent in many families. Indeed, I had a privileged childhood – not in material things, but with love and all of the spiritual blessings that cannot be bought with silver and gold.

With this background and a personal commitment to Jesus Christ, how could I write a curriculum that might blur and negate God's intentions for the family? Yet I knew that this family life area represented widely divergent and conflicting opinion. What content should be included? How could a Christian develop a curriculum that could include topics of teens using condoms, exploring homosexuality, drugs, and abortion? The agenda before me frightened me and I wondered what influence, if any, I could have for good.

My first inclination was to ask for a change of assignment, but whenever I was ready to discuss my concern, I felt a subtle prodding of the Holy Spirit encouraging me to accept this task. It seemed as though the childhood I had was so beautiful that I would be wrong to deny that influence to the curriculum opportunity before me.

With relatives and friends praying for me and this initiative, the project began. Before the final selection of names for membership on the curriculum steering committee, I placed every name before God in prayer. I believe it was God who selected that committee. Together we agreed on a set of core values as the foundation of the curriculum. They were the values C.S. Lewis wrote that the Bible intended for society: honesty, empathy, commitment and self-management. The committee and I felt that the more controversial topics of masturbation, abortion and homosexuality should be left to the family, and we left that out of the curriculum.

Our unit promoted abstinence from sexual intercourse as the best choice for young people. We designed a lesson that was to help students develop skills in resisting peer pressure and saying no. Integrating God's principles in the work was a difficult task and the road was not always smooth. At one time, my supervisor asked me to include a lesson showing both sides of the abortion question. A draft lesson was written but I felt it was out of place. Again, more prayer. You guessed it – the committee felt it was not compatible with the document and threw it out. At this point I quit worrying and just started believing in earnest that God would see me through.

Meanwhile, the relationships with my committee and co-workers often found people directing their family problems to my desk. It is a very sensitive situation, but you can direct people to a good church for help in those settings. I look back now at one committee member who grasped that there was an absolute, sure road map for the course of her life in the principles of the Bible. She went to the church I recommended, became a Christian and today is a beautiful illustration of a woman building a family on a solid foundation.

The curriculum was completed, released and implemented. Parents from the Christian community were sceptical about a provincial curriculum in family life education. The more liberal lobby groups mocked the content as "a head-in-the-sand approach." Newspaper headlines ridiculed its effectiveness.

As parents reviewed the document, however, support across the province became widespread. Today, requests for the curriculum come from all across Canada and the United States. Parents and educators are looking for materials that stress the importance of family and that promote abstinence as the best choice for young people.

TRAPPED BY THE CULTURE

*Former prime minister Brian Mulroney once said to a visiting
Italian president that first-generation Italian-Canadians built
Toronto's skyline and the second generation owned it. That is an
exaggerated claim, but not a misleading one, says Luciano Del Monte.
But he finds that though materialism may have permeated the
culture of his people, many Italian Canadians are looking for
what money cannot buy.*

Rosetta and I are first-generation Italian-Canadians who met
and fell in love in an Italian language class. We are among the
half million Italians who live in the greater Toronto area. Our
people are hard-working and generous. Our social lives centre on
family and food, and we are explosive in our spontaneous
responses of emotions and loving. Our people are also good at
making money.

Still, the Italian experience has not been free from deep pain.
This has been attested to by Franca Carella, former director of
social services at Villa Colomba in Toronto. Well-experienced in
dealing with the Italian-Canadian community, she said, "The
degree of psychosomatic illness is really very concerning. We
must do something about it."

She went on to say something that would probably not make
her popular among Italian-Canadians.

"The trauma of immigration," she said, "is only one part of
the reason for all of this. There is something else. There is something missing among too many Italians. They came here in the
1950s with a vision – making money and owning a house. They
got the house. It became a castle. Then they gave their children
everything they never had: clothes, cars, trips. But too many for-
got that while we were wearing five-hundred-dollar boots on our
feet, our heads and our hearts could be empty. What about the

inner person? We are forgetting the emotional (and spiritual) needs of people." [1]

Well, Rosetta and I were part of the Italian community looking for something to put in our heads and hearts. Through the friendship of Navigator staffers Brian and Martha at the University of Western Ontario, we came to Christ. They were careful not to get into debates with us about denominational issues and distinctives. They always brought the issue around to who Jesus was and what He wanted of me. I finally invited Christ into my life when Brian explained Revelation 3:20 to me, "Behold, I stand at the door and knock."

Jesus told a man who had been converted, "Go home to your FAMILY and tell them how much the Lord has done for you, and how he had mercy on you" (Mark 5:19). That has been an important focus for us; we have sought to go to our family first and bring them to Jesus – not to a particular church, but to Jesus. We are thrilled to see family members coming one by one to know Jesus.

—— 125

Influenced by churches that were culturally biased, at times we felt pressure to become Anglo-Saxon more than to be Christlike. We got the message that to be true followers of Christ, we had to stop drinking wine, stop dancing, stop going to the festivals that had been part of our formative years, and so forth. Bringing Italian friends to church backfired because of this cultural issue. I have come to agree with Joe Aldrich, president of Multnomah School of the Bible, who says, "The greatest barrier to evangelism is not theological but cultural."

As we have been enabled by the Lord to lead many of our

---

[1] *Canadese; A Portrait of the Italian Canadians*, Kenneth Bagnell, McMillan Canada pg. 244-245

Italian friends to Christ, we have asked them to teach us. The majority have made it clear that they are uncomfortable in Protestant, evangelical circles, as you can appreciate because their roots and cultural identity are very much engrained in Catholicism. But they love the ambience of a kitchen table, being with people like themselves, where Bibles are opened, and needs are shared and prayed for. In these settings our friends discover that religion is not an outward system but a relationship with a living Christ.

This journey has meant that Rosetta and I and a number of friends and family who turned to Christ have banded together to reach our people. In 1990 we became full-time Navigator staffers, supported by faith donations, mostly from our people. During a quiet time, the Lord impressed us with God's word from Esther. As Esther reflected on her people, the Jews, she said, "For how can I bear to see disaster fall on my people? How can I bear to see the destruction of my family?"

We began to refocus ourselves so "our people" would now become the Italian-Canadians. We are slowly seeing the barriers of our Protestant identity come down. One day, while we read about the freedom we have in Christ in a living room full of Italian-Canadians, one of them blurted out, "If this is true, then there is hope for my parents. They can be won. Until now I thought they could come to Christ only if they joined the Baptist Church." Imagine a Baptist Jesus, or Presbyterian, or Anglican, or Mennonite, or Navigator or "whatever" Jesus!

There are wonderful conversion stories happening among our people and through some of these emerging "oaks of righteousness" we see emerging communities of believers in Woodbridge, Guelph, Niagara Falls and the west and east ends of greater Toronto.

POLITICALLY CORRECT

*Patty Bowman loves politics but believes that just because a Christian
is called to an office, one's faith does not necessarily make
all insights accurate. Rather, it only gives the person the responsibility
to fear God and attempt to apply His love on behalf of the people
that politician serves. As a school board chair in one of Canada's
most populated school districts, Patty has plenty of opportunity
to "walk that talk." She is responsible for spending almost a
million dollars a day and she also believes she has a "system-wide"
responsibility for evangelism.*

The crux of the evangelistic focus I pursue hinges on this one thought: that God's righteousness should be established in all and through all. I expect righteousness from my friends and colleagues – both those who do and those who do not profess Christianity; and I simply attempt to force that end by calling forth the need for constant provision, care, nurturing, love and truth for the individuals we are responsible for.

Let me give you an example. Some time ago, one of our students wrote to the board requesting condom-vending machines in high school washrooms. Deeply troubled over this request, I shared my thoughts with my colleagues and tried to put into words the ache in my spirit. It was the one and only time I have come to tears publicly in nine years of board business. Sitting in my chair, all I managed to get out was, "The need of our young people is much deeper . . ." and I started to weep.

I lost the position I sought at the board committee level; however, one of my trustee colleagues sent a card of encouragement as the issue headed to the next level of decision making.

As I recall, the card read, "On Monday evening when you feel like you're losing the debate, look over at me and I will smile to reassure you. Do your best . . . as I know you will." It was signed by Louise, the leading voice in opposition to my position.

My opponent tried to encourage my voice of protest. This was all I needed. I stood up inside, dusted myself off and lobbied hard. The following Monday, I did what she suggested. I took my turn in the debate and looked for the encouragement she had promised. Sure enough, there she sat, smiling and nodding her head in affirmation.

The vote was taken and the decision of the committee was overturned. The position I had originally lost was now supported. Though I was pleased to win the debate that day, I will never forget the challenge Louise provided me. She does not profess Christianity, but she challenged me, by example, to love the individuals I work with while still debating their convictions. She reminded me that I can call out for righteousness to be established in all and through all, and still be characterized by a spirit of love.

I have come to realize that love is the garment we wear in public office. There are countless encounters where this has led to a verbalization of my faith and to times of prayer, as friends come to embrace the Lord of love.

You see I am not called to politics; I am called to Christ. I am called to his heart, to be near Him, to daily reflect His love for the world. I use the vehicle of community leadership, but my dream is to touch the lives of real people with real change. It is a privileged calling we have as Christians; we are free to love in the natural and the spiritual and to carry in our frames the love of Christ. It is a privilege to be shared.

"TEAPOTS ON FIRE"

Though she once thought that being a Christian artist meant painting pictures of Jesus all the time, Lynne McIlvride-Evans has discovered other ways to cultivate a relationship with God in paint.

A picture about the size of a child's puppet theatre hangs in a public gallery in downtown Toronto. Spiky, silver-haired characters splash and swim and jump through the water like energetic elves. Words of prayer jump out of the characters' mouths while they battle against waves or walk triumphantly on top of them. Such are the visions of Lynne McIlvride-Evans.

On another gallery wall, heavenly creatures cavort through the air, holding on to technicoloured haloes. The Lion of Judah stands with milk-filled teats and soul-melting eyes. "Come to me all who are thirsty" reads the text, curling like a vine round the frame.

Lynne McIlvride-Evans is thirty-two, a successful professional artist and a Christian. She sits for eight hours a day in her studio on a dairy farm in Uxbridge, Ontario, and cultivates a relationship with God in paint.

"When I first dedicated my life to Christ at sixteen I was interested in art," explained Lynne. "I thought, in a rather immature way, that I'd have to draw pictures of Jesus all the time. I tried to make Him a contemporary Jesus, one who fit into my teenage surroundings, by putting Him in T-shirts." When she studied fine art York University, she began to realize that God could use her work for witness even if it carried only a subtle message.

"Quite early on in my course I was inspired by Amish quilts. I realized that they were made in some way to God's glory, even though there were no pictures of Jesus sewn on. That was when I first started to realize that you could show your faith in subtle ways. For instance, the diamond shape on many of the quilts was a symbol of Christ," she explained.

It was a Marxist professor at York who taught Lynne not to be shy of expressing the things that are closest to her.

"He was very generous about my Christianity," recalled Lynne. "He taught me not to be afraid of expressing strong beliefs in my art. I use a lot of metaphors in my paintings and sculptures."

To illustrate, she points to a picture in another corner of the gallery. Bright, fiery flames carved from wood burst out from under the lids of painted china tea pots, and fire and rainbows pour out of their spouts.

Tea-pots on Fire is the depiction of God's presence filling human vessels, explained Lynne. "Ordinary, clay vessels filled with the Holy Spirit," she said with a smile.

Today, the curators who select Lynne's work for galleries and exhibitions throughout Canada and the United States praise her for the integrity, as well as the quality, of her work. Her style has been described as medieval primitive and her painting has been compared to that of Marc Chagall and Georges Rouault.

Biblical texts are written into the frames of many of her paintings: Christ healing the man's ear in the garden of Gethsemane; Christ raising the little girl from the dead.

The two-word verse, "Jesus wept", is painted under a cut-out figure drowning in a sea of words. The piece is titled, *Church Lady Drowning in Patriarchy*.

"The words are an added layer, not an explanation of the painting," explained Lynne. "Because I'm a Christian, people assume that my art is message oriented. But I just want to express what is inside. And because part of what is inside is Christ, hopefully that comes out.

"I see the world as very rich and multi-layered, but also fallen. So my art is about this, in both content and materials. I use layers of paint and broken objects. So I'll make a face out of broken glass and bits of china and bright paints. Not because people look like that, but because people are like that."

In this way, Lynne's art has become a journal of her relationship with God and part of her expression and journeying with Him. Many of her prayers have been hung from gallery and church walls across the country. Many more hang in the homes of art collectors and art critics.

Whatever fame continues to come Lynne's way, one thing is certain. She will continue to pour herself out in a fiery, rainbow-coloured vision to challenge Christians and unbelievers alike.

■

WHAT'S REALLY
IMPORTANT

Everyday life confronts us with tough choices. With so many competing calls for our attention and resources the struggle to maintain a sense of priorities is an ever-present reality. It is easy to lose our sense of balance as we try to juggle all the demands being made of us. The real key is to ask God for discernment and wisdom in establishing what is really important. What we see and identify as important is all a matter of perspective. What is His perspective?

For instance, what priority do Christians place on the challenge to move outside of the walls of the church to become actively involved in the lives of those who do not yet know Christ. One of the producers of *As It Happens,* a CBC radio news analysis show, expressed it well, "Please, get your hands dirty in the debate and don't just shout at us from the sidelines, telling us we're all wrong. Get in on the issues; wrestle with how we'll solve these problems; give us a thinking presence of the Christian world. Get in on the debate."

God needs more "Hidden Heroes" who will make it a priority to enter our society with a credible presence and witness for the gospel by becoming engaged in the issues facing our culture. Don't expect this to be an easy path to take. In fact, the Christians who are most effective in evangelism have friends who are committed to prayer on their behalf, spending time together, keeping each other accountable for the priorities they have chosen by God's grace. The higher your priority is to penetrate our unreached culture, the stronger your commitment must be to nurture your relationship to God and His people.

Take encouragement from the stories of those who have chosen some very clear priorities and have seen God at work through their efforts.

— dm

FROM

ANOTHER

PERSPECTIVE

People who don't know God and the way he works fuss over these things, but you know both God and how he works. Steep yourself in God-reality, God-initiative, God provisions. Don't worry about missing out . . . Give your entire attention to what God is doing right now.

Matthew 6:32-34 (TM)

VANDALS, VICTIMS, VICTORY

*In 1982, reporter John Longhurst had an exciting assignment. He was
to travel Europe and interview eighty new Christians about how and why
they converted to Christianity. After a year of research and interviews,
he documented that only three of the new believers had accepted Christ
when they first heard the gospel. The remaining seventy-seven could
look back and see times when God nudged their hearts through an act of
kindness by a Christian, something a Christian said or just the way
Christians lived their lives. For them, the road to Christ was marked
by many little experiences. Longhurst calls that activity "pre-evangelism"
and he is committed to fostering that action. As media director for an
international aid agency, Longhurst encounters dozens of folks he regards
as Hidden Heroes in pre-evangelism – people who do not explicitly or
verbally call others to conversion, but who point the way to Christ. Here
he opens his files and shares a couple of illustrations.*

In 1976 Elvera Corben of North Vancouver was an emergency
room nurse. One night a single mother and her two children were
rushed in with gunshot wounds. The mother and her twelve-year-
old daughter were wounded; her fourteen-year-old son was dead.
On finding out that the mother had shot them and herself
because she felt overwhelmed by the pressures of being a single
parent, Elvera decided she must do something to help women like
her.

The result was the Open Door, a ministry for single mothers. It
started in Elvera's home before moving to Hillside Baptist church
in North Vancouver. The ministry offers child care several mornings a week so mothers can go to various appointments or just get
a break. Volunteers provide support, friendship, counselling and
Bible study.

"The goal of Open Door is to introduce single mothers to
Jesus, to a whole new way of life which is not destructive," said

Elvera. But, she added, "it's not good enough to only go to church. [The mothers] need to feel good about themselves. They need to develop parenting skills. They need to have loving relationships with men without having sex."

Elvera launched into the work full time and assisted more than half a dozen evangelical congregations to start an Open Door in their churches. For Elvera, meeting the various needs of single moms is her way of sharing Christ.

"Evangelism is not just something you do – it's how you live. Our care for others shows who Jesus is."

* * *

In 1974, two Elmira, Ontario youths went on a one-night vandalism spree causing more than $2,000 in damage. They were

arrested, charged and faced incarceration. When Mennonite Central Committee staff persons heard about the case, they wondered if it would be better for the youths to meet their victims, receive forgiveness and be restored to the community. They called this restorative justice, taking as their example God's desire to restore people to Himself – without ignoring the sin.

They persuaded the judge to let them try it. Together with the youths they visited all twenty-two victims of the vandalism. The youths expressed their sorrow and promised to pay for the damages. Many of the victims were surprised to see them; some expressed anger, but others showed genuine concern.

Three months later these young people went from door to door again – this time with a cheque for each victim. As a result of the experience, the youths felt they could hold up their heads in the community, and the victims felt something had been done to make things right.

Christians are called to be lights in the world. That light shines through actions like those in Elmira. That pilot was the tool to launch victim-offender programs in many communities all across North America. It is injecting Christian values of dealing with wrong, forgiveness, restoration and making things right.

Heroes like these show our society that the church is vitally involved in meeting needs across the country. And when we do that, we suddenly have a beautiful entree into mainstream society.

■

COURTROOM DRAMA

Judge Ralph Carr believes in the Nehemiah principle. Nehemiah was cup-bearer to King Artaxerxes, and as such had a unique perspective from which to win the king's support in rebuilding the walls of Jerusalem. "We are all Nehemiahs with respect to someone — a dad, a brother, people who are part of our life, whom we can impact," Ralph says.

— 139

From his perspective, Provincial Court Judge Ralph Carr says the courtroom is a dramatic, exciting place to be. Christian faith has a bearing on his sense of justice, he says, because "the precepts and principles of the Bible speak to the notion of justice."

Having a practice in criminal and family law until his appointment to the bench three years ago in Timmins, Ontario, it was easier to share his faith directly in the work environment. It is important, he explained, to be sensitive to others while maintaining a certain amount of intermingling of the professional and the personal.

"I am who I am. If I am fair and I am just and if people see me as being a humble person, I give the credit to the Lord," he said.

Ralph holds up as his goal Micah 6:8: ". . . what does the Lord require of you? To act justly and to love mercy and to walk humbly with your God." (NIV)

He strives to live out that verse in his profession. If at the end of his life it could be said of him that at least that was the direction he headed, then, he said, "I would consider my life to be a success."

He says his father was governed by Micah 6:8. It was the combination of his parents' example and the claims of the gospel that led him to make a personal decision for Christ at the age of eight. Even at that young age, he realized he needed the presence of Jesus Christ in his life, "not only for life everlasting, but through the ups and downs of earthly experience."

His desire to share his faith grew out of the realization that Jesus Christ is not a theological abstraction but a real and living person, and that salvation is not earned but is a gift that must be accepted by each individual.

"It seems only reasonable and natural to share that with others who need the Lord," he explained.

That natural desire has led to many opportunities. In one case, a successful lawyer who was experiencing a lack of peace in his life asked him about his faith. He spoke freely of his need and questioned Ralph about his Christian beliefs.

Ralph was able to share with him that happiness and contentment are not found in "material success and professional achievement." He also told his colleague that "happiness does not stem from a complicated analysis of any point of view or philosophy of life, but is contained in a person, the Lord Jesus Christ." Although that man never made a decision for Christ, others have.

Ralph is also involved in community outreach. With the support of his wife Diane and their five daughters, he helps to organize Christian sports outreach banquets, where high-profile

Christian athletes are brought in to speak at a community event.

He also shares his faith at banquets and other occasions, including speaking to the Toronto Blue Jays. He believes his life and faith are summed up in Proverbs 3:5,6 " "Trust in the Lord with all your heart and lean not on your own understanding; in all your ways acknowledge him, and he will make your paths straight." (NIV)

■

"ON DUTY" OFFICER

Ever since the start of his law-enforcement career fourteen years ago, Bruce Day's fellow officers have been aware of his Christian faith.

The officers-in-training were told on their first day that they were to come prepared the following day with a five-minute story on any subject. "The first thing that popped into my mind was 'I'm going to tell them how to become Christians,' " recalled Bruce Day, forty-five, a police constable in Winnipeg.

When it came time for his turn, "the place was dead quiet." Afterwards, one of the other officers came to ask him more.

"Right from the second day on the job, they knew Bruce Day was a Bible thumper. I didn't chase people, I didn't bug people," he said. But when they asked, he shared his faith.

That reputation as a Christian has led to both harassment and opportunity. Early in his career, two sergeants "just hated my guts." After a couple of years, he was ready to quit. Instead, he prayed about it and was transferred to a different department.

Whether training recruits or responding to calls, Bruce has been "up-front" about his beliefs. When he was engaged in the field training of recruits, he and his wife Sandra would invite the new officers to their home for a meal and a time of talking together.

A non-aggressive approach with his colleagues has for the most part earned him respect.

"They accepted the religious part of me because it was on their terms," he explained.

A few years ago the Winnipeg police started a chaplaincy program to respond to some of the personal needs of police officers (the separation and divorce rate among police is seventy percent) as well as community people. Bruce was invited to become one of two police chaplains – an invitation he sees as a miracle – and given training for his new role at Providence College. The Winnipeg force became the first in Canada (followed by Calgary) to have active police officers as chaplains. The chaplaincy program required ordination through his home church, so Bruce is now in the third year of an ordination process with the Evangelical Free Church.

As chaplain, Bruce wears an identifying cross on his police uniform. His chaplaincy duties mix with his job as a community police officer in a storefront office. The label "chaplain" has given him opportunities and freedom to talk to fellow police officers who ask for help, as well as answer questions from the people he meets on a daily basis.

When a staff-sergeant suffering from leukaemia was transferred to a Winnipeg hospital from Regina, Bruce began dropping in on him to chat. "He didn't want any part of me."

After several visits, Bruce stopped by one day when the staff-sergeant was alone and "at a pretty low ebb."

"I came to apologize," Bruce said. The staff-sergeant asked what for.

"I said, 'I have the answer to life, and I haven't told you.' " Bruce had talked about sports, weather and other "peripheral things," but not about God.

"I asked if I could share something with him." The officer agreed. After Bruce explained how Christ died for his sake, he asked the staff-sergeant if he would like to receive Jesus as his saviour.

"He said yes. Tears were rolling down his face."

As soon as the officer had prayed to invite Christ into his heart, his wife walked in. When he told her he had accepted the Lord, she told him she had just done the same, through a Women's Aglow meeting.

The staff-sergeant, a "strong, silent, rough, tough" man, died last Christmas. His story illustrates the key behind Bruce's approach: "meeting them where they're at and giving them the answer – the real answer." —— 143

Being a chaplain means Bruce can officiate at weddings, a job he relishes.

"I get to talk to non-Christians," he explained. During pre-marital sessions, he asks the couple about their own beliefs, gives them the Jesus video to watch, presents them with Bibles, and, if they are open, tells them more about the Lord.

In most cases, there is no immediate interest in making a Christian commitment, but Bruce believes that at "some point down the road it's going to take hold."

Being open to sharing his faith springs from a vital personal relationship with God. "I meet with God every day," he said. "I get up and I know He's waiting for me, and I meet with Him."

One officer, "one of the foulest policemen" in the department, recently ask to meet with Bruce. Looking around to see if anyone was listening, he confessed, "I accepted the Lord." The officer had gone to his wife's pastor when he felt he could no longer live without God. Having made a commitment, he had to share the news with someone who would understand. "I was the first person that he told."

■

DEATH THREAT

Rita Koosees lives on the northern fringe of Canada at Kashechewan on the coast of James Bay. Ten years ago, Rita, along with her husband Alex, became a Christian. Since then they have been released from alcoholism and had their marriage restored. Amazed at the change in their parents, their twelve children and two foster children, aged six to thirty, have all responded to the gospel of Christ. Their oldest son is in Bible school and Rita witnesses to the power of salvation through church ministry, her teaching job and on a regular radio program.

144 ——

I am a forty-eight-year-old First Nation Cree from northern Ontario and God is using me to reach my people with the gospel of Jesus Christ.

My life before Christ was one of despair. Though I attended a Roman Catholic residential school as a child, I was thirty-eight years old before I discovered the Bible. I feared God, but didn't love Him or know Him.

I am grateful for the education I received from the nuns in Fort Albany, even though I rarely saw my parents from age six to fourteen because they were on the trapline while we were in school. They wanted us educated because the traditional way of life wouldn't always be there.

Our marriage was happy at first. But after our third or fourth child, my husband began drinking and cheating on me. I would catch him and ask him to come home. He would abuse me. I became addicted to Valium in my search for release from anxiety, and I too started to drink because I was bored and unhappy.

Recently, the Lord spared me from a man with a shotgun who wanted to shoot me to avenge his mother's blood. The native police constables arrested him with the gun. He was the son of a woman killed many years ago by teenagers on a shooting spree. My daughter spent two years in prison because the police found her wandering around the next morning with a gun, high on drugs and alcohol. They never found out who did the shooting.

My husband was one of the ten people shot that evening. I was living with another man at the time. Desperately unhappy and tired of being a battered and abused wife, I had left my husband and children two years earlier. When my husband was shot and flown to the hospital, my children went to live with my married daughter in Kashechewan. My husband urged me to dry out for the children's sake and I did. We got back together and drank once in awhile but not as before.

— 145

We had been given a house in Kashechewan and I started going to a little church across the road, called Faith Pentecostal Temple. For a year I went to the church before giving my heart to the Lord on Nov. 1, 1984.

I felt the joy of being forgiven because I knew I was going to hell. It took many years to heal our marriage. I had to learn to forgive my husband, even though he too was now a Christian and truly a changed man through the work of the church.

In August, 1991 I decided to go to the National Native Bible College in Deseronto, Ontario. My husband and our children who were still at home moved with me. It was a wonderful time of being trained in the Bible.

Now back in Kashechewan, I have been in charge of the Sunday school and am training three women to teach along with me. Children whose parents are unsaved or backslidden are hearing the gospel through this ministry. I also go on the northern radio to share the gospel for two hours on Saturday and Sunday mornings, sharing the gospel in both Cree and English.

During the school year I teach Cree to students at the public school on the reserve. The students sometimes ask me why they can't make me angry or why I'm so happy. Of course, I tell them. They will also ask me questions about being a Christian.

God has also opened up a counselling ministry for me. People in the community know my story. They have seen the changes in my life. Before I became a Christian I was a wild woman. I didn't care what I said to anybody.

146 ——— I tell people the truth about my life and show them kindness and acceptance. I want them to know that God is no respecter of persons. I share with them the message of Philippians 4:13: "I can do everything through him who gives me strength." (NIV)

■

HIGHROLLER WITH A HIGH TOUCH

"I witness to others about God's love, not because of how He saved me from great difficulties, but because of how much He has blessed my life, long before I even knew Him personally."

For twenty-five years Michelle Bertrand has had an enormously successful career in sales in Montreal; she currently owns her own finance company.

When Michelle was twenty-five years old, deep into a destructive lifestyle, and she thought suicide was the only way out, someone opened the door to a career in sales. Even then, she knew this came from God. She discovered she had vast talents in approaching people and selling products. By the time she was forty, she had a new husband and everything she could possibly desire materially.

She felt empty. Emptiness led to panic.

One night, in 1984, she visited a client at home and observed that the woman owned next to nothing. While they worked out a long-term plan for buying certain appliances, the client emanated an internal serenity that Michelle found deeply disconcerting. Soon after, the client sent a letter, saying she was praying for Michelle. No stranger had ever shown that kind of love to her before. After this woman shared the gospel with her, Michelle began to attend a new church, where she accepted the Lord. —— 147

Immediately she began to experience dramatic changes. Instead of using every minute to sell, she found herself lingering in people's homes to share the gospel with them. Money became less and less important to her. At the same time, her new pastor observed her thirst to lead others to Christ and he and the elders thought she should take the Evangelism Explosion course. She went away to pray about this and felt that God confirmed to her that she had a special gift of evangelism and was calling her to this ministry.

She took the course and describes the outreach.

"We went door to door. I had no trouble going into strangers' homes because of my career. Soon a large number of people accepted the Lord and our church was filling up."

Her life's testimony has had a great impact on her family as well. Following the example of the woman who witnessed to her, she often writes letters to loved ones. As she explains, they can reread the letter and respond thoughtfully.

"They take it more seriously than a phone call."

Her family has especially noticed her perseverance in her Christian faith. After watching her for three years, her husband also became a Christian. Then her brother Robert followed and her sister Marie-Luce.

"My sister saw so much change in my language and my behaviour that she could not resist following my example." Even her mother-in-law, a bitter, sad woman who came to live with them for the last year of her life, finally accepted Christ six months before she died.

Currently, Michelle is praying for, writing to and witnessing to her step-son and her nephew. After years of total rebellion, both are taking giant steps toward salvation. "This alone is a miracle and a reward for my patience," Michelle said

Because she has regular clients that she works with over a long period of time, she has many opportunities to share her faith. She is careful how she "mixes business with witnessing," and never wants to make people feel uncomfortable.

"With my Muslim clients, it is very delicate." But even when sales are not good, God brings people along to whom she can witness. She has a simple strategy. "Everywhere I go – the bank, the notary, a boutique, a client – I ask God to open doors. And He does." Right now, two of her clients have begun attending her church after they received Christ with her.

Recently, she attended a viewing at a funeral home. The room was filled with people. As she sat down, the woman next to her struck up a conversation and they discovered they had much in common. The following night Michelle went to the woman's home and shared the gospel with her and they will continue to meet together. "It often happens like this to me."

Because of her financial success, Michelle has many friends and contacts in "high society." She hosts receptions in her home, to which she invites both Christians and non-Christians. She shares her testimony and they are often amazed that she sees God as the one responsible for her success. Last year her church sponsored an evangelistic supper for Valentine's Day. Of the sixty-four people she sent personal invitations to, nine came and one now attends her church.

Her greatest challenge is to know how to divide her energy between sales and her ministry of evangelism. To give up an evening of sales to visit the woman from the funeral home, for instance, took discernment and discipline. But her greatest joy is having the privilege of being present when someone accepts Christ as Saviour.

"My pleasure in life is right then – when another becomes a Christian."

■

DOWNSIZING BRINGS A BIGGER DREAM

"Downsizing" is a buzzword everyone hears but hopes will not apply to them. When it happened to Ron Bales after twenty-eight and a half years with the same company, he and his wife Pam wondered how God could use them.

At noon on November 4, 1991 my husband Ron called me at home to ask for prayer. He was about to meet with his boss, and he had an uneasy feeling about the summons. Pray I did.

At 4 p.m. Ron called me again: "I've been given a month to clear out my desk." When I asked how he felt, he replied that it was like a door in his life had been closed.

"God must have another plan for me now," he calmly stated, "and we must pray to learn what that plan is." And pray we did.

How did I feel? Two years earlier, when downsizing began to affect some of our friends, I thought this would never be my problem. Ron was upper management – secure. But over the past few months, as we took our nightly walks – our one opportunity in our busy lives to keep in touch with each other – Ron had been gently preparing me for the possibility of just this situation.

Now we were unemployed, and the thought was actually exciting. For years I had dreamed of us being in ministry together. I don't think I had resented Ron's job, but I had regretted that it consumed so much of his time and energy. Because he had used his God-given talents to the full in the business world, God now had given us some free time to seek and serve Him. Ron's pension, we decided, would be adequate to live on.

Over the next few months, opportunities to work with eight different Christian organizations came to our attention. Our nightly devotions together grew into a real seeking of God's will for our future.

For many years we had been sensitive to the needs of young people, and have had ten teens other than our own four children live with us for periods of three months to three years. Seven of these youngsters were unable to remain in their own homes because of family breakdowns, and two of them were pregnant. Our own children have been very supportive in sharing their parents, home and possessions with "other people's kids" or "OPKs", as they have called our temporary residents. As I write this, we are into the second generation, for the young woman now living with us is the daughter of our first OPK, who lived with us in 1969.

Would youth work of some sort be in our future? I believe that God has gently led us in this direction. Through my involvement with our Christian school as a board member, and our daily prayers for its survival, Ron became aware of the school's needs. Less than three months after his "golden handshake," Ron's gifts with numbers were being used to assess the situation and forecast the future of the school. Six months later, he offered himself to the school for a year as their full-time volunteer administrator. That was two years ago, and although other opportunities have arisen in the interim, God's plan for Ron still appears to centre around the Christian school.

We've gone on to enjoy the fruits of a home Bible study and as a result have seen several of our friends come to a personal faith in Jesus. We've worked as team members in various crusades in Canada and overseas, and enjoyed a number of home ministry opportunities. Incredibly, I overlooked evangelism for almost thirty-five years, but am delighted that we could discover this vital part of our Christian walk before it was too late.

—— 151

■

Engaging Exuberance

Aimee Stolte admits she sometimes gets nervous about sharing her faith, thinking her friends might ask her some of the "really tough questions" about whether God actually exists. But in her young life, Aimee has proven to be a consistent, caring friend whom other kids come to when they are ready to accept the Lord.

At fourteen, Aimee Stolte is already a veteran when it comes to inviting her friends to share her Christian faith. The grade nine Saskatoon girl has seen three of her friends come to the Lord.

Aimee likes to invite her friends to Sunday school, youth group or summer camp.

"When I started going to youth group," she explained, "I didn't want to go alone, so I started to bring some of my close friends. Then other people wanted to come."

Packing out her parents' van and another car, Aimee holds a local record for bringing her friends to youth group. "I think the most I brought was eleven."

Confident and outgoing, Aimee is not shy about explaining to her friends what God means to her. "I just go to my good friends and say, 'There's this neat youth group event going on. It's in the church and we do lots of fun stuff and they talk about God after the games and how the games relate to God.'

"At first they just come for the games because they don't know much about God."

Aimee is being raised in a home where faith – and sharing it – is important to the whole family. Her parents, Eric and Marion Stolte, set the example.

"They taught me that God wants to use me," Aimee said, "and I shouldn't hide God or anything. I talk to them about stuff like that."

"We encourage [our children] to be lights where they are," Aimee's mom explained. That means friendships are built not only at school and youth group, but at football games and school dances.

Aimee has found that after her friends start hearing about God at youth group or camp, they often ask questions. One young friend who went with her to a girls' club wanted to respond to the leader's invitation to accept Jesus into her heart. But instead of asking the leader to help her, she asked Aimee.

"She asked me if I could pray with her. We did it in the bathroom," Aimee reported, adding, "We were just getting a drink." She was eight or ten when that happened.

Does sharing her faith come naturally? "With some friends it's easy, some friends it's not," she said. "Some friends don't really listen to that kind of stuff, so they're harder to talk to."

In those cases, she is sensitive about how much she says and when. "If they don't seem interested, I'll leave it for a while."

"Sometimes I can get nervous," she admits, "thinking they'll ask really hard questions."

And they do. Like, "How do you know that God is real?"

But even if she has a logical answer, "it would be hard for someone to believe in God right away."

Aimee finds she needs to work at keeping a balance. Though she does not want to be too aggressive, "you don't want to really live in secrecy."

Her personal relationship with God is important in preparing herself to share her life and faith. "I like to pray because it makes me feel more confident." Reading the Bible and learning more about it at Sunday school and Bible study also help.

IN SPITE
OF THE ODDS

"Church Youth Killed on the Way to Bible Quiz Meet." The headline screamed out across the newspapers, radio and television. How could this happen? Where was God when this took place? Not only were they innocent but they were committed to His Word, which was the focus of their quiz meet. Yet through this tragedy a number of young people gave their lives to Christ Out of that same tragic root began the Dallas Valley Ranch Camp (named in honour of one of the dead youths), which has become one of the largest and most effective youth camps in Saskatchewan today.

As the fabric of life is woven, we do not see the attractiveness of the final product until the last stitches are completed. Only then can we turn the fabric over to see what has been hidden during the weaving process. With a totally different perspective, we can then see the wisdom in the steps taken by the weaver to produce such a piece of exquisite beauty.

— 157

There are countless "Hidden Heroes" across Canada who recognize God's sovereign hand at work in their lives even though they serve through circumstances that defy human explanation. When everything seems hopeless and discouragement sets in, they lean on God's unfailing love and seek His face for strength and courage to go against the odds. He remains true to His promises and never fails to answer, providing the essential hope needed to carry on. The recognition of His ultimate purposes are sometimes realized but often His purposes are accepted by faith that He is in control.

– dm

When everything was hopeless, Abraham believed anyway, deciding to live not on the basis of what he saw he couldn't do but on what God said he would do . . . Abraham didn't focus on his own impotence and say "It's hopeless. This hundred-year-old body could never father a child." Nor did he

FROM

ANOTHER

PERSPECTIVE

TOO YOUNG TO DIE

Life was rolling fast for Gilles and Jeanne LeBlanc. Their family-owned lobster and crab processing company in Cap Pele, New Brunswick employed more than 250 people and recorded annual sales of twenty-five million dollars. Along with their partnership in a restaurant and an embryonic mussel operation, Gilles was finishing a thesis for his master's degree in engineering. They were expecting their third child when their daughter Jani was diagnosed with Acute L Leukaemia three days before her first birthday. Excerpts from their diary tell the story of the days that followed.

November, 1987. A rush of questions flooded our minds . . . Why her? What caused it? Is it our fault? Why would God do this to a beautiful innocent child? Our entire world changed upside down.

September, 1988. Jani has relapsed three times and her only hope for long-term survival is either a bone marrow transplant or a miracle. Initial tests indicated that none of our family members match to donate marrow.

January, 1989. We believe God is going to heal Jani as we learn that our new baby boy Mathieu has perfect compatible bone marrow. Because of Mathieu's age, the transplant has to be performed in Boston.

February 3, 1989. Transplant day. They're going to harvest Mathieu's bone marrow in the morning. . . . We will have to sit tight and pray and wait to see if the transplant will successfully engraft.

April, 1989. The transplant was deemed a success and Jani is, in one doctor's words, cured.

Wednesday, September 20, 1989 5:00 a.m. Jani woke up screaming in pain. She's suffering intensely. Jeanne gives her Tylenol and codeine but she throws it up. Jani is dying. . . . It's very difficult for us. We feel as if God has abandoned us.

10:30 a.m. We are at the hospital. . . . Jani has not regained consciousness since last night. She still cries regularly. God is showing us that He has not abandoned us.

12:30 p.m. Start giving morphine to Jani. It calms her immediately.

11:00 p.m. Jani is resting peacefully but it's as if she is in a shell. She is not the same Jani. She has not regained consciousness since last night.

Thursday, September 21, 1989 3:45 a.m. Jani has thrown up a lot of old blood. She is now sleeping peacefully.

Friday, September 22, 1989 3:00 a.m. Jani suddenly wakes up and starts talking to us, smiling, etc. It's the same Jani. It's a MIRACLE. GLORY TO GOD! Psalm 138:2,3,7,8.

Saturday, September 23, 1989. 1:00 a.m. Jani is so active. I can't get her to sleep. She wants to walk in hallways, play, draw, etc. She's a bundle of energy. Glory to God for having "raised" Jani (Hebrews 1:10 -14).

Wednesday, September 27, 1989. Jani comes home from hospital. Our families are very touched by Jani's miracle.

Friday, September 29, 1989. Around supper time Jani becomes violently ill. Her pain is so acute she clutches and scratches our faces in desperation as we hold her in our arms. It is very difficult for us to see our little baby suffer so much. We turn to God in prayer knowing that her physical and eternal life was entirely in His hands. Now that we realize that maybe a cure is not God's will for Jani.

1:13 a.m. October 1st, 1989. Jani died.

Though it was extremely painful to lose our precious daughter, a unexplainable peace came over both Jeanne and I as God gave us an assurance that He was in control and that somehow Jani's short life would be used for His glory. God sees each of our lives from an eternal perspective and, in a sense, whether we live one day or a hundred years is relatively insignificant if God uses that life to bring others into His kingdom. How did He use Jani in that way?

We learned later that Jani's illness was bearing witness to Christ in several ways we did not realize. For example, an acquaintance of Jeanne's who had to spend Christmas in the hospital due to her son's asthma attack was feeling very sorry for herself. Jeanne went to visit to encourage her, and Linda was profoundly touched by Jeanne's courage and positive outlook in spite of having to spend the whole year in the hospital with a terminally ill baby. This began a searching process that resulted in her becoming a Christian.

A second example is Jeanne's close friend Norma who had been very annoyed at hearing us say that Jani's life was in God's hand and His will would be done. She could not understand why we were not mad at God for what was happening. The night of October 1 Norma was preparing refreshments in our kitchen for both families who had come to our house to offer their support. Christian music was constantly playing on our auto-reverse cassette player that we had forgotten we had turned on. Norma was curious and listened carefully; the Holy Spirit was working in her heart and she asked us the meaning of some of the words. We gave her a Bible and for a couple of weeks after that Norma would often call and ask questions about the meaning of various verses. Soon she became a Christian.

During this time, God was giving Jeanne and I a burden for the people drawn to us through Jani's death. We decided to start a Bible study in our home following the approach in *Your Home a Lighthouse* by Bob Jacks. With much help from our friends Ken and Judy Anderson, many lives were touched through this. Over the next four years, more than fifty people attended at one time or another, and close to twenty of them have become Christians. This has had quite an effect on our small, close-knit Acadian community of 2,000 people. For example, in Norma's case, her husband, daughter, four sisters, one brother and several friends have come to Christ. Our next-door neighbour who, before becoming a Christian, would walk in front of our house during our studies in hope of being invited, finally invited himself and subsequently became a Christian along with as his wife and two teenage sons. We are into our third Bible study now and we are seeing a healthy body of Christ emerge from the pain which began with Jani's illness.

■

FROM RICHES TO RAGS

162 ——

Young-Wha Kang (not her real name) was a reluctant immigrant to Canada in the 1970s. But since then God has drawn her out from a sheltered life to befriend homeless people in Toronto.

In 1975, Young-Hee Kim's husband decided to move his family here from South Korea so he could make his fortune. Over the next nineteen years, that goal became the wedge that finally splintered the couple's fragile marriage.

"My husband came here to establish his future, and I came as a humble wife and mother," said Young-Hee, a freelance artist who has four children and has been separated from her husband for the past three years.

"After we moved, I cried for years because I was a very shy and private person. And people aren't that way here."

But Young-Hee wanted to obey her husband, so she tried to make the best of her new situation. Though the money he made in Canada was good, and she enjoyed being able to buy almost anything her heart desired, she knew something was missing in her life. That "something" turned out to be a deeper relationship with Jesus Christ.

"After the birth of our fourth child, somehow our finances went wrong, and problems really came into our lives," said Young-Hee. "Our marriage was shaky because my husband wanted to move to the States. He wasn't satisfied here. Our children were against that move, and I was caught in the middle."

Young-Hee decided to fast and pray to find God's will about where she should live. Two weeks later she noticed a sign advertising an open house. The custom-built, $800,000 home attracted her, and she quickly made an appointment for her husband to see it. He fell in love with the house, and it became theirs in 1989.

But even though the Kims loved their home, it was not enough to hold their marriage together. Young-Hee's husband eventually moved to the States to pursue his financial dream, and she remained in Toronto. Instead of feeling bitter, she has turned her tragedy into a ministry by witnessing to the many people who ask to see her home's beautiful interior. —— 163

"I've had a lot of people come through this house, and it is my testimony that my God is not a small God," she said. "People admire the house, and I tell them it belongs to God, and I'm just renting it. I've shared my testimony with about 100 people. I have no training in evangelism, but I leave everything to the Lord. I like to be used for His glory.

"God has used my weakness, and now I have real confidence through Jesus. Before, I was always afraid to speak out. As I grew, I wanted God to use me in a quiet way through my art. But He has forced me to open up and talk to people, and has given me the strength to be able to do it."

Young-Hee also incorporates art into her testimony. Each Christmas, she displays a large hand-painted manger scene in her front yard. She plans to put up a painted Easter scene this year that will feature a large wooden cross. Her purpose is to show people how Jesus came to earth and died for them, she explained.

Recently, Young-Hee's ministry has expanded beyond the borders of her home. Because of her youngest son's prayers for homeless people, she became aware of the street people in Toronto. When that son visited a Christian summer camp that focused on reaching the homeless, she realized God was using him to call her to a new ministry.

"God gave me a heart for these people, and they seem to be attracted to me," she said, and explains that she has visited a downtown Toronto street mission every Tuesday evening for almost a year. There, she listens to the mission's visitors and tries to encourage them. "I tell them that God loves them, and we pray and cry together."

Young-Hee also helps to feed many of the homeless people she meets at the mission. Last year she cooked Thanksgiving and Christmas dinner for them. And she regularly helps serve donuts, coffee and hot dogs to the people. For her, it is an opportunity to show Jesus' love in a tangible way.

Young-Hee estimates that about 150 street people have come to know the Lord through her ministry. But she is quick to point out that the credit belongs to God.

"I'm really nothing," she said. "I can't even speak English well. It's Jesus in me. I'm not here for my own future – I'm here to pay Jesus back for what He's done for me."

■

FROM CRIPPLE
TO MARATHON RUNNER

Is it possible to evangelize the press? Mark Fetherston, a Winnipeg man who loves to jog, certainly thinks so.

It was Friday night and my wife and I were out for a spaghetti dinner with a few friends. One of them recognized an acquaintance in the restaurant, a sports reporter who happened to be sitting nearby. The reporter came to visit our table and mentioned that she was covering the Manitoba Marathon. I was training to run in this marathon and I immediately felt an eagerness in my heart to witness to this reporter.

When I was introduced to her I said, "Hi, I used to be a cripple." She laughed, but soon was amazed at my story. Just two years ago, I told her, I was unable to walk because of rheumatoid arthritis. I was in such pain, I had to be carried to the bathroom.

Through a venture to a school of evangelism in Florida, I was miraculously healed and I told this reporter I anticipated running thirteen kilometres in the upcoming marathon. Meanwhile, my wife dug into her purse and showed the reporter a handy testimonial letter written by my doctor, stating how he could not medically explain my recovery. We carry this letter with us in faith that God will provide opportunities to share His goodness.

The reporter was intrigued and wanted to cover my story. Two days later, when it was time for the marathon, she was there with camera man in tow. The result was a beautiful article in the *Winnipeg Free Press* under the headline, "Man claims prayer freed him from pain, former invalid's recovery 'miracle'." It told readers province-wide how powerful God is and what He did for me.

I am continually amazed at what God can do through our testimonies when we are prepared to boldly act on the opportunities He presents to us.

—— 165

MIDLIFE INTENSIVE CARE

*Despite being paralysed and confined to a hospital, Kathy Harvey has
found that God's strength is enough for every situation.*

For twenty-eight years Kathy Harvey has been the prisoner of
an unresponsive body. But although Multiple Sclerosis (MS) has
affected her voice and paralysed everything except her neck, head
and vital organs, the fifty-three-year-old former nurse has not let
the disease stop her from reaching out to the people around her.
In fact, her weakness has become a vehicle to tell others about the
availability of God's strength to everyone.

"I like to present myself as an example of how the Lord can
use any life and open doors with it," said Kathy, who has been a
resident at Mississauga Hospital for sixteen years. "Recently, I got
to speak to a class of gerontology students enroled in a university
course called 'Religion, Spirituality and Aging.'

"I couldn't say much about aging, but I was able to present a
talk on the subject of the dignity of personhood from a hospital
resident's point of view. A question came up about where I got
my strength, and it was the perfect opportunity for me to talk
about the Lord and how He has sustained me."

That's a subject Kathy understands from experience. Her initial
MS symptoms occurred when she was a teenager. Then they disappeared, so the disease was not diagnosed until the symptoms returned when she was twenty-six. MS causes the body to gradually
lose its ability to move. At that time Kathy was working as a nurse
as well as caring for a husband and two children. Once again, the
symptoms disappeared, this time until she was thirty-two. Within
two years Kathy's movement became restricted to a wheelchair.
Four years later, she was a permanent hospital resident.

For Kathy, the most difficult part of that long experience was
the pain of leaving her family.

"This disease hits most people when they're most needed – between the ages of twenty and forty," said Kathy, whose children were eleven and thirteen when she was hospitalized. "But God has given me a wonderful family, and they've included me in everything. I've been able to remain an active member."

As she adjusted to the changes in her life, Kathy began to look for ways to establish friendships and share her beliefs with other patients. She learned speech therapy, and was soon encouraging stroke victims twice a week as she taught them to speak again. These sessions gave her opportunities to present her testimony.

Also, because of a strong desire to receive spiritual nourishment even in her isolated surroundings, Kathy started to listen to Christian radio and television programs in her hospital room. As the nurses cared for her daily needs they were exposed to these programs and began turning to her with questions about what they heard.

About six years into her stay at the hospital, Kathy noticed a man painting with his mouth. Someone asked Kathy if she would be interested in learning that technique. She was eager, and by 1985 was so skilled at mouth-painting that she was commissioned to paint an annual Christmas card by the Mississauga chapter of the Multiple Sclerosis Society. Since then, she has painted other Christmas card scenes that reflect her spiritual viewpoint. One oil painting, entitled "Endurance," depicts a slender tree standing firm as the wind buffets it. And her "Place of Refuge" oil painting features a quiet, snowy scene dotted with barns, trees and a small, wooden shack.

But Kathy said that her greatest opportunity to influence other lives for Christ is through her role as patient advocate. She has served on several health care reform committees, and is also president of the hospital's residence council, a group that links staff and patients. In each setting, she is a living testimony of how God empowers people to perform tasks amid personal weakness.

"I look at my disease as an opportunity," said Kathy. "I have more time than the average person, because I don't have the stresses of life that they worry about. I have more time to read God's Word and pray here. And I can talk to people who are hurting, whether they're staff or patients."

■

SOUTH PACIFIC PRAISE

Freda Cooper and her family know the price of following Christ. Their lives are threatened by active spiritual resistance to the gospel. But Freda also knows that she has the strength and grace she needs for each moment.

Several times a year Freda Cooper hosts teams of young people from the South Pacific at her home on the Tsartlip Reserve near Victoria, British Columbia. Their aim is to reach out to people on Vancouver Island; their preparation is prayer.

"What I think is needed here on this reserve is praise," said Freda, sixty-two. Explaining that her people, the Coast Salishan, have been engaging in the same spiritual practices for many generations, she said the teams that spend time on the Tsartlip Reserve lift up the name of Jesus to replace the powers of darkness that bind the reserve.

Freda's firm Christian beliefs have made her unpopular with her neighbours. A few years ago she was leading Bible studies

with several young people from the reserve who had accepted
Christ. The spiritual leaders on the reserve did not like it. They
kidnapped two of the young people and took them to the long-
house, where physical and emotional punishment, blindfolding,
isolation, hunger and brainwashing are frequently used in an initi-
ation process to give a person a spirit power.

When Freda tried to protect the young people by harbouring
them in her home, she came under siege. For months, her house
was surrounded by men who would stare through her windows
and run up and down her steps, and in other ways try to intimi-
date her.

The relationship she found in Jesus twenty-five years ago has
given her grace to endure each hardship as it arises. A love of
reading since she was young led her to turn to Christian books
and to the Bible when she was searching for answers after her
father's death. Although she talked to no one, she began to understand the concept of being born again.

"There comes a time when each of us must confront who Jesus
is: Who is this man?" One night when she could no longer escape
the conviction, she knelt down and asked Jesus into her life.

A working mother with six children, Freda had never found life
easy. But the real onslaught of hardship came after she made a
commitment to Jesus – including losing a son who was murdered
in 1973. "The Lord has seen me through, and through all this
there has been a strengthening which cannot be removed."

Freda has kept a low profile on the reserve in the past few
years. She acts as an informal consultant to Victoria churches, providing counselling and prayer for new native Christians, especially
those who struggle with their pasts. She hosts outreach teams.
During the Commonwealth Games in 1994 more than a dozen
members of a group called Teams Reaching Out from Pacific

Island Churches stayed at her home. She also holds a summer Bible school for children in the area.

She still experiences persecution. "It amounts to stalking," she said. Sometimes in the mornings, she finds evidence of witchcraft outside her house – a medicine wheel or bundles of rocks tied up in cloths placed around her house. "These are curses," she explained. To combat their power, she prays around her yard.

"Most Christians don't realize the power of witchcraft and curses done in ritual," she said. "Most Christians don't realize this can kill. And that's the whole intent here."

Only once was she afraid. One night she woke up to hear owls hooting right outside her house. Because she lives near the road and away from the forest, "I rarely even hear an owl hooting from the forested area. For them to come down to this cleared area is very, very unusual.

"With my people, owls are associated with death. They are the curse of death."

When she heard the owls, she went to the door and yelled at them to leave, in the name of Jesus. Birds generally are frightened away when someone approaches them or speaks. "They just got louder. They hooted louder and louder."

Freda went back in the house, knelt down and began praying for every member of her family, her children and her grandchildren. Then she prayed for all her Christian brothers and sisters. "When I got to the very last name I could think of, the hooting stopped."

About a month later her youngest son was out partying when he decided to come home early; he didn't like the way his friend was driving. That night the friend and his passenger were killed in a head-on collision. For days afterwards her son sat in the house saying, "I should have been in that car." Freda sees incidents such as this as attacks on her family. Danger is forestalled only by prayer.

People have asked her why she does not leave the reserve. But she believes she belongs there and that leaving would be compromising. A pastor once asked if she would be willing to lay down her life for the Lord.

"I didn't have an answer. I said I don't think we can know that." Peter, she pointed out, said he would give up his life, and then he denied Jesus.

"But one thing I do know, that if the Lord requires that, then He will enable me at the time by His grace. Not before the time, either. It will take place at the time of danger."

Jesus has always provided her with the strength and grace she needs for each moment, she pointed out. "And that's what we can count on."

■

— 171

REALITY WITH
REBELS AND RIDERS

There is not a dry eye among a crowd of teens as Alain-Pierre Pelletier compares his life on the street to a trash can in front of him. What can the power of God do when a man has reached the end of his hope?

To the blaring music of Guns 'n Roses, a man in ripped jeans and a muscle shirt staggers on stage, an empty liquor bottle in his hand. In vain, he tries to throw the bottle into the nearby trash can. He falls on the park bench placed centre-stage.

As the music changes to the haunting strains of Franz Liszt, Alain-Pierre begins to speak of his private hell of drugs, drunkenness, loneliness, rejection and his constant desire to end it all in suicide.

The audience that fills the sanctuary sits rapt by the dramatization of his life story. More than half in the room are not Christians, including the whole front row of thirteen- and fourteen-year-olds from a local Christian drop-in centre. They do not move a muscle as he describes being so stoned that he did not even feel a bullet that hit his shoulder. They understand what he means by "feeling all alone."

It has been many years since Alain-Pierre was eighteen and living on the streets. Now in his late thirties, he and his wife Marie have been walking with the Lord for a dozen years. He works for a furniture manufacturing company in the Laval area, north of Montreal, and is the chair of his church's evangelism committee. Because he has come far under God's hand of grace, it is his foremost desire to lead others to Christ.

Still a free spirit, he walks the fine line between the rebels he touches through his ministry, and his whole-hearted submission to Christ and the leadership of his church.

"I can reach people for the gospel that straight people in churches could never reach," he said.

The monologue he delivers about fifteen times a year is one program of three he has developed to share the gospel. Sometimes he joins a Christian band for an evening of music and testimony. The third format touches on the other passion of his life: motorbikes. He and other members of the motorcycle gang God's Disciples put on evening outreach programs for churches.

One pastor in St. Jerome, Quebec invited Alain-Pierre to present an evangelistic program. He brought along members of his gang. When the church members arrived, they had to pick their way through the motorbikes and leather-clad visitors to find the door and their seats inside. But that evening the church was packed and there was an atmosphere of fun. Many stereotypes, both about "straight"

Christians and "rebellious" motorcycle types were put to rest. One young man named Philippe, whom Alain-Pierre had brought along, gave his life to Christ that night. The success of that evening has been a catalyst for more outreach and renewal at that church.

Since acquiring a classic Harley-Davidson, Alain-Pierre is a welcome client at certain other gangs' garages for repairs and service.

"These are not the kinds of places you can hand out tracts," said Alain Pierre, as he explained the need to take it slowly when it comes to witnessing among the biker crowd.

The approach is different than the dramatic stage testimony where he illustrates his life change of finding hope and salvation through faith in Christ. On those occasions, Alain-Pierre comes forward to his audience on his knees, reaching to heaven with outstretched arms.

Many have joined his challenge to come to God for salvation — 173 For many others, his vulnerability in showing that God is able to redeem the broken brings them one step closer to the kingdom.

■

CARING ENOUGH
TO COMMIT

If history could be replayed, we would find plenty of "Hidden Heroes" who have significantly influenced our communities across Canada. Individuals who went "the extra mile" often paid a great price and made a significant impact for the kingdom. Don Page, vice-president of Trinity Western University in Langley, British Columbia, relates the story of two such heroes from the early days of our capital city. Before Queen Victoria named the city Ottawa, it was called "Bytown." It would never have been chosen as the capital had it been the old Bytown. Bytown before 1867 was one of the most despicable towns in all of British North America.

It was a town in which every fourth building on the main street (Rideau) was a tavern. Every night saw main-street brawls in which at least one person was murdered in cold blood. The riots left many dead on any given night, including Sunday, — 177 because the taverns were open seven days a week, twenty-four hours a day. Into that milieu came the Irish, English and the French, who were there for agriculture, lumber and building the canal.

There were two men who were determined to do something about the Bytown situation: Nicholas Sparks, a Protestant, and Daniel O'Connor, a Roman Catholic.

Their vision was to be God's ambassadors, and they came together to pray about what to do. As God led them through their prayers, they began to preach the message of reconciliation among those tough Irishmen, Englishmen and Frenchmen.

Within a matter of months, Bytown became peaceful. As a permanent memory to what those two men had done, Sparks Street and O'Connor Street intersect in the form of a cross, pointing toward Parliament Hill.

Such sacrifice and dedication mark the stories that follow. Each reminds us that a complacent Christian is a contradiction of terms. In fact, we are reminded that all it takes for evil to triumph is for good men and women to do nothing.

– dm

FROM

ANOTHER

PERSPECTIVE

But there is another urgency before me now. I feel compelled to go to Jerusalem. I'm completely in the dark about what will happen when I get there. I do know that it won't be any picnic, for the Holy Spirit has let me know repeatedly and clearly that there are hard times and imprisonment ahead. But that matters little. What matters most to me is to finish what God started: the job the Master Jesus gave me of letting everyone I meet know all about this incredible extravagant generosity of God.

Acts 20:20-24 (TM)

Messianic Mail Messages

Gideon Levytam, thirty-nine, of Niagara-on-the Lake, Ontario has a
passionate hobby of mailing out Bibles in plain paper packages.

When I met Irene, a beautiful girl working on a kibbutz in
Israel, she was the first person to tell me in any measure about
Jesus Christ. I had no interest in Jesus. But I certainly had an
interest in Irene, and fell in love with her. After I immigrated to
Canada and spent time with Irene and her gentile Christian fami-
ly, I became more exposed to Jesus.

I was offended when Christians presented the gospel to me. I
felt that because I am a Jew, if anyone should tell others about
God it should be me. After all, I am one of Abraham's people. But
I discovered that these gentiles knew more about my God and my
people than I did and I was impressed by this Messiah they talked
about. Irene's mother offered me a Hebrew Bible and wanted me — 179
to read it. I took it, but said I would not read it because it included a New Testament. Nor would I enter their meeting place
because I was afraid it would be wrong, and, generally speaking, I
was afraid of their symbol, the cross.

One day, Irene's mother asked me to help her vacuum at their
church. I agreed and sneaked in the side door, afraid of what would
happen to me. That was my first time in a church. Gradually I began
to feel more comfortable and began attending meetings there. I discovered that Jesus was a Jew, and the New Testament was written by
Jewish people. But it continued to be a real battle for me, and it
took about three years for me to fall in love with this Jesus.

There was an older Christian man who invited me for supper
and gave me a New Testament. He was a wonderful person. He
really loved me and showed me slides of Israel and of believers
there. This time I did read the New Testament, and once I realized
that Jesus was the Jehovah of the Old Testament, I simply went

home and knelt and prayed, "God of our father Abraham, if this Jesus is truly the Messiah, than I want Him in my heart."

That was 1980. My appetite for life began to change completely. I had an urge to make much of the Messiah. I began to get up at 4:30 a.m. just so I could read the Bible and meditate. I have done that for years now and that's what gives me strength to share Yeshua at my work.

I am a boat builder, a carpenter, very similar to the Master, but I work in a factory making fibreglass yachts. I began to read my Bible at coffee and lunch breaks and one day, a Portuguese man I worked with asked, "Are you a Jew?"

I said, "Yes, but I am one who believes in the Messiah." I gave him a Bible and he began to join me as we studied the Bible at lunch, then another joined us and both have since gone on to be baptized and join our church. Every day, we still read our Bibles and pray together at work.

I may have been bold in sharing Jesus with the gentiles, but to share Him with Jews was a scary thing. I was asked to distribute Scriptures to Jewish people, and I struggled with that call. Yet I knew that it was the word of God that had reached me, that it affects the human heart like nothing else, and so I felt at peace to enter this work.

After my hours building boats, I now send Bibles to Jewish homes across North America. My church supports this work, and there is no cost to the recipients. We send out 100 Bibles a month, about thirty of them are returned by Jews who want nothing to do with the New Testament; they send very discouraging letters sometimes. However, I pray Romans 10:17 for this work, that faith will come by hearing the word of God.

Not long ago, I approached my boss and asked for Thursdays off so I could do a Bible study with Jewish people in Toronto that I have come to know through my witnessing. He said yes, and I am happy to go. It is a loss of a day's wages, but on that day I am building something really worthwhile. I take the train to the Bible study so I can rest and prepare as I go. Both believing and non-believing Jews attend this study.

I should tell you that Irene did marry me, even though I was not a Christian at the time, and she now cares full time for our three sons. I have been homesick for Israel and because of that our boys all have Jewish names – Shalom, Joab, and Nathaniel. Shalom just had a Hebrew-Christian *bar mitzvah* as he turned thirteen. It was a special time of blessing him for becoming a man. We had 100 people in attendance and it was a beautiful opportunity to share the Messiah with our friends and Jewish family. We blessed Shalom with a passage from the Old Testament and one from the New Testament and an eighty-eight-year-old Jewish believer gave the message. It was a wonderful celebration. —— 181

■

SILENT WITNESS BY BIRTH

When the Yorgey family goes to Montreal prisons to minister each Sunday, it is twenty-one-year-old Marc who people come to see. Though he cannot speak, sit up or eat on his own, Marc Yorgey has touched the hearts of many people around Montreal – including his own family – and he has been a witness to God's grace and love across Montreal, especially to people in prisons. His parents, who have cared for him for all of his twenty-one years, have been his mouthpiece.

Years ago, Jim and Roma Yorgey were full of hope, like any new parents who dream dreams for their firstborn. But at six months, when Marc still could not roll over or hold up his head, they knew something was terribly wrong. Finally, when Marc was eight months old, they got the devastating news that he had severe cerebral palsy. Roma was already expecting the first of their two daughters – Sara and Janna.

But God graciously unfolded His plan for this family to lovingly embrace Marc. And His daily miracle of grace proved to be a witness to the unloved and forgotten in society.

Jim and Roma have been missionaries in Quebec with Christian Direction, Inc. for more than twenty-five years. Jim has spent most of these years visiting men daily inside the walls of several prisons around Montreal. He shares his faith, disciples believers and lends a listening ear. For sixteen years, the Yorgey family has been going regularly on Sundays to conduct chapel services for men in prison. Although the Yorgeys' ministry of music and the Word has been greatly appreciated, many of the men can relate most to Marc. Just as Marc is handicapped by his body, they too feel handicapped by their prison bars. Yet, when they see the deep love this family has for Marc, it helps them grasp the deep love God has for them.

Though Marc is handicapped, he does not feel like a prisoner of his body. Jim explains, "Unlike the prisoners behind bars, he is not frustrated. He is truly a happy person." This message speaks louder than any words.

Their life with Marc has not been easy, yet Jim and Roma can truly thank the Lord for their special responsibility. "Marc is a gem," said Roma. God's kingdom has grown in the hearts of many through Marc Yorgey's silent witness to His grace.

GOD: A FRIGHTFUL CONCEPT

*In the heart of Vancouver's downtown, Granville Street comes alive
at night when musicians, street kids and drug dealers line the sidewalks.
Among the crowd is Shannon.*

"The kids seem to find it comfortable talking to me. My skills
in terms of relating seem to be toward adolescents and kids my
own age," said Shannon, a woman in her early twenties who left
her university setting, and let her heart pull her to disadvantaged,
poor and uneducated Canadians.

What she began to see on the street were kids with gruff, often
rage-filled exteriors. "It's astonishing to see what is hidden inside
these kids. It became a challenge for me," said Shannon.

Accustomed to seeing street workers come and go, the
"streeters" were surprised when Shannon stuck around. She is now
in her fifth year of caring for the Granville neighbourhood.

— 183

"Kids see a lot of street workers burn out on the street. When
you stay, they want to know why," said Shannon. With another
Christian friend, she opened a house for street kids. One of the
first boys to move in was a homeless teen named Luke.

"The main thing for him was, 'Why?' " said Shannon. "He
wanted to know why we hung out with kids who kept us awake
all night. Luke was someone who asked his own questions. He
would come to our Bible studies and ask what makes God real?
What makes God more real than native spirits?"

She began to show him that God can be personal, and began to
explain how Jesus brings that about.

Luke lived in the house for more than a year before moving
out. He is now off drugs and off the street but is not yet a
Christian. For street workers, evangelism often comes in much
smaller steps than immediate acceptance of Christ, said Shannon.

"The most difficult thing was learning not to take responsibility for things that I can't change. I'm learning that if I overstep my bounds I build an unrealistic relationship with the other person and ultimately that will be destructive," said Shannon.

She listens more to God these days about what she should – and should not – be doing for the kids. She prays constantly, almost always in some kind of a discussion with God in her head.

The number one thing she tries to show the kids is unconditional acceptance.

"What some people find as comforting – God as Father – is a very frightening concept for these kids, most of whom come from dysfunctional families," explained Shannon. "Their idea of love is not based in anything concrete. For them it doesn't have anything to do with being taken care of or being valued."

Evangelism to street people, said Shannon, has a lot more to do with what you do than what you say.

■

SIGNED ON FOR A UNIQUE CALL

Losing a job can be a terrifying experience. But for thirty-year-old sign painter Bernard Racicot, God turned it around into an opportunity for a ministry of evangelism.

In 1992, Bernard was the highest-paid commercial sign painter in his shop. He was also the employee who complained the most about his boss's under-the-table transactions. When the recession hit Montreal, he was the first to go. Although he had always been a hard worker it was a tough time to be hired elsewhere. He and his wife Nathalie, who had one child and another on the way, prayed for God's direction.

It had been while preparing for a career in graphic design in CEGEP (community college) that Bernard met a group of Christians with GBU (French-language IVCF) and accepted Christ. The open home/open heart approach of GBU worker Pierre Baillargeon touched a familiar chord with Bernard. From the moment of his conversion, he wanted to reach out to others in a nonaggressive, accepting way.

Realizing that he enjoyed ministering to kids more than to adults, Bernard applied for and became the director of the new Centre Accroche, a Christian after-school homework and drop-in centre for teens in St. Laurent, Quebec. The centre is open afternoons from three to six. Once teens visit the centre, there is no pressure on them to come back. But forty or more kids did come back on a regular basis during the 1993-94 school year. Bernard's greatest desire is to see this group of teens accept Christ, and he has the patience to stick with them until they do. — 185

Bernard still accepts sign-painting contracts to help support the centre. But the greatest adjustment to his new career is that he is employed for who he is and not for what he can produce. This was freeing, because he does not have to make products for a deadline, but stressful at the same time, because his character and his spiritual maturity play an important role in his work. He still works hard, happy to use his talents and his open-hearted approach with people in a Christian setting.

The kids especially like it when Bernard brings out his guitar or when they go to hear his band perform an evangelistic concert. They talk with Bernard about spiritual things, and he hopes that when they have problems they will come to him first. He has already proven to them that his door and his heart are open.

Translating Talk Into Walk

Like a pied piper, Jim Jacobson can be seen every week with a collection of
children trailing along with him, on their way to an important event.

Spending time with a roomful of boisterous kids is not everyone's idea of unwinding after a day at the office. But for Jim
Jacobson, a translator with the Manitoba government, it's the
highlight of his week.

Jim leads a weekly club called Know Your Bible. Each
Wednesday he leaves his downtown Winnipeg office and knocks
on doors in a core area neighbourhood (he spends lunch time
doing the same), inviting local kids to come to the half-hour club.
Attendance averages about thirty, with as many as fifty or sixty
coming some weeks.

When Jim, now fifty-three, started the club in 1989, he was not
sure where he would hold it. But he went around knocking on
doors; if parents asked where the club would be held, he explained
that he did not have a place yet. Families keen on seeing the club
go ahead eventually agreed to allow it in their homes. And the
children followed him around, telling him where other kids lived.

"They were enthusiastic," he said. "In their own kind of guile-
less way, they helped out." Twenty kids showed up the first week,
and the number has rarely been less than that.

The half-hour club includes singing, a ten-minute Bible lesson
or story, prayer, and a lunch of sandwiches and milk, prepared by
volunteers from Bethesda Church, where Jim attends with his wife
Bettie. In a neighbourhood that has serious social problems,
including alcoholism, violence and poverty, the sandwiches stand
in for an evening meal at home for some kids.

Those who attend are anywhere from three to thirteen, most
between seven and ten. Eighty percent are aboriginal. Many are
from single-parent homes.

Jim's impact is not limited to the short time he spends in club.

"A very significant part of this whole thing is what happens in homes," he explained. Sometimes parents, who are encouraged to attend themselves, are open with him and want to talk about their problems or have him pray with them. Through the home contacts he has also been asked to visit relatives or friends in hospital. And always, when he makes his rounds before club, there are children in tow.

Reaching out to others has long been part of Jim's life. He used to hand out tracts on Main Street. People he met started telling him about their children and the problems they had. He decided his efforts would be better directed at the children. He remembered attending a club called Know Your Bible when he was a boy, and decided to start his own club. He led the first one for a few years before dropping it because of other responsibilities. He started the current club five years ago and leads it throughout the year, including summer. Both his son and daughter, now grown, have been involved, as well as many other volunteers.

——187

Although he can become discouraged when the kids are rowdy or make excuses not to come, or when he witnesses family problems, Jim has never been tempted to drop the club.

"It's the highlight of the week for me," he said. "Sometimes I feel almost closer to heaven in these situations than I do in church."

Having the opportunity to tell others about Jesus makes it all worth while, especially when they respond. One girl accepted the Lord near the beginning of the club five years ago and, now fourteen, is attending a Christian school. Her father has also become a Christian, as have other adults with whom Jim has come into contact through the club.

Sometimes parents will be uninterested or even rude. Jim continues to be friendly, and they usually warm up eventually.

"You have to be perseverant without being importunate," he explained. In one case, two little boys were forbidden to come back to club after they heard a lesson on the devil. "The mother was quite upset because you shouldn't talk about the devil." Jim prayed and waited.

One day he had to hold the club in a back yard when the hosting house was not available. The two little boys were watching over the fence. Soon they were allowed to go back to club, and both have accepted the Lord.

■

Cutting to the Heart
of the Community

Not content to be a forty-watt bulb in a room full of fluorescent lights, Val Martens has become immersed in her unchurched community so that her light may shine in the darkness.

The community of Rundle, in northeast Calgary, is diverse in race, religion, language and culture. There is a wide range of social and economic levels among the population of 12,000. There are five schools, lots of children and young families, but only one church.

Val Martens hopes to change that. The thirty-six-year-old mother of one has been busy doing research to find out the needs and interests. When her daughter started kindergarten shortly after the family moved to Rundle six years ago Val began to realize that this was a community without a central Christian focus.

Val and Woody Martens had earlier made a decision to cut back on church commitments in order to be more available to their neighbours. Through volunteering at her daughter's school Val was able to meet people and build friendships in an easy, natural way. As leader of her local Moms In Touch prayer group, she also made contact with the school administration and found their positive response encouraging.

A tireless worker, Val spent many volunteer hours, along with her husband, campaigning for a local candidate in the federal election.

"This provided opportunity to witness by our lifestyle but also a few opportunities to actually share verbally what being a Christian really means," she said. She also worked on committees that allowed her to get to know her local school trustee and alderman. In each case she worked at maintaining a positive and supportive role.

Involvement in her community has made Val think about the importance of a Christian influence.

"The closer I get to seeing the world's issues and concerns through the eyes of those around me – especially non-Christians – the more I realize the desperate need to bring Christ into my community in a very real and tangible way."

Several of her non-Christian friends were "extremely loyal supporters and dedicated workers" when Val ran as a candidate in a 1993 aldermanic by-election. Sometimes that meant one of them was present when she gave her views on a moral issue while campaigning, which led to further conversation.

Seeing social needs in her city, Val helped recruit Christian workers for a youth drop-in centre. Two teens have since become Christians, and others have been introduced to church groups.

— 189

Not one to dodge a challenge, Val approached her church growth committee a couple of years ago with the idea of planting a church in her part of the city. They gave her the go-ahead and some funding to research the area. To assess her community's needs, she met with social workers, principals, police officers and other community leaders.

"I really think they were honoured to have been asked for input," she said. They all indicated they are "more than willing" to work cooperatively with a church body that meets real needs of the people they are also serving.

She has also knocked on doors, taking a survey to find out interest – with surprisingly positive results.

"A lot of people who don't go to church at all showed a positive attitude."

190 ——— Whether the church meets initially in a school gym or a strip mall, Val's vision is to offer practical help in response to people's needs. That could mean holding seminars on parenting skills, budgeting or conflict resolution, or offering help to single parents. Or it could mean teaching English as a second language to new Canadians.

"There's a real need for ESL classes," she explained, especially with recent funding cuts. "I think churches have missed the boat by not being more prepared."

Though she has no intention of being pastor of the new church – her gifts are in laying the groundwork and establishing relationships – Val wants her light to shine in the community.

"I don't want to be just another forty-watt bulb turned on in a room full of fluorescent lights, where the impact is unseen or unnecessary," she said. "I'd rather be the light bulb that shines brightly in a dark place, and makes people long to bring more light into that same situation."

■

THE MOST UNDESIRABLE STREET

*Wade and Penny Kovacs had their hearts set on life in a log home far
from the city. But they gave that hope to God, and He led them to an inner
city neighbourhood where a pellet gunshot through the dining room
window was the calling card of the new "welcome wagon."*

When Wade and I married, one of the things we had in common was love of the country. We had both grown up in small towns, and felt that a rural setting was the perfect place to live and bring up children. Our first home was in Winnipeg, but it was a "white picket fence" type of setting in a quiet neighbourhood.

Through a variety of circumstances we met Harry, a pastor who had just moved to Winnipeg from New York with hopes of starting an inner-city church. A fledgling Bible study group meeting in his home grew to the point that he knocked down his living room wall to make room for the session. When it grew that large enough that Harry considering starting Sunday services, our choice to make this tiny house church our home was an easy one. I had visions of seeing our small group that we called New Life multiply quickly. I dreamed of going into the neighbourhood helping people, feeding the poor, encouraging those caught in harmful habits to change their lives.

I did not suspect it would be I who would change. I saw the city as a scary place, especially the inner city. When the pastor from our old church, after listening to our plans to attend New Life, asked if we would be moving into the area, I must have just about laughed in his face. The idea was so ludicrous and so foreign to our thoughts that we didn't entertain it for a minute.

After a few years, we became a bit disheartened with our work at New Life. We would just get to know someone and they would move or stop coming. Attendance was sporadic. We would see people make life-changing decisions and slip back into their old patterns as we watched helplessly. In many ways, I was no different, wavering from deep faith in God to wondering if He even existed or cared.

Wade and I made a firm decision to move to the country, and started building a log home about 90 miles out of Winnipeg, close to relatives. I was looking forward to the freedom my children would enjoy – the fresh country air and wholesome life.

During this time, Wade was fairly discouraged with his job and life in general. He was finding some enjoyment and sense of accomplishment, however, in building the log home. I remember him saying that the only thing that would keep him in the city was if the church took off.

That year it happened. Attendance grew to about forty to fifty on a typical Sunday. A number of dedicated Christians joined our team, and excitement for our work increased. God was at work, and spiritual renewal swept through us. That summer Wade and I decided to stay.

Then, because New Life had a proven track record with helping its neighbourhood, the church received a large government grant to erect a new building. Thrilled with this development, we worked hard at completing an actual church building for New Life. It is a beautiful, useful facility that enables us to now open during the week as a drop-in centre, with our main meeting room doubling for Sunday services and a daily coffee shop. We were able to volunteer there and meet more people from the community. Through the drop-in centre and events such as church-sponsored block parties, more people began attending Sunday services.

Wade and I had the needs of the church and its community in our hearts, but we were also part of the neighbourhood we lived in and had relationships to give attention to there. On top of that, our kids were attending a language school in another area, and we wanted to develop and maintain contact with parents of our children's friends, as well as have input in the school. We began to realize that zeroing in on one community would simplify our lives, and make us more effective. Moving to our church neighbourhood would enable us to meet the people who did not have cars or phones. We would actually be members of the community, instead of people on the outside. Our caring, while just as real before, might be seen by some as more believable, because problems in the community would now be our problems as well.

Our decision to move to the inner city was not made lightly. Naturally, we had some very real concerns about moving our children into a neighbourhood known for its high crime rate and substance abuse. We worried about moving them from an stable school to one with a transient student population and where the value systems of some of their classmates might be vastly different from what they had known. I will not pretend that my concerns have disappeared, but my prayer is that these new situations and experiences will be used for good – to develop in our children qualities and attitudes that are positive and will strengthen their relationship with God.

One of the things I found hardest about moving was the negative reactions we got from many people – even Christians. "You're moving where?" "Are you crazy?" In fact, our new address has been termed by many as "the most undesirable street in Winnipeg." These comments did not make me want to change my mind, which I see as further proof that this is where God wants us.

In our minds, the blessings of our new inner-city home far outweigh the sacrifices we have made. For instance, we live across the street from our church and drop-in centre. My children will grow up seeing their church trying to make a difference, being involved in their community and school. The multicultural exposure we receive here is sure to be rewarding. We have good friends here, and a large old house that is a handyman's delight for Wade and a decorator's dream for me.

I have seen the beauty here – in the large, leafy trees that bow their heads over the street, in a lovely flower I noticed by our front step, and in the many faces that pass by every day. For a neighbourhood labelled "hopeless" and a people that have "given up," these growing things speak to me of hope and possibility. For me and the other members of our church who live in the area, our prayer is that God will use us to share His love with those in our neighbourhood who desperately need a new chance.

Now we have been here almost a month. Shortly after the bullet through the living room window, Wade's Moped was stolen. We found it vandalized in the back lane. We are pretty sure we know who did it – not hardened criminals, but elementary school kids. These children are bored, neglected and angry. They are our neighbours – part of our outreach area.

Will we make a difference here? I don't know. I do know that God has made a difference in us, and I feel better just trying.

■

A SEARCH FOR DEEPER ROOTS

As a nineteen-year-old in Manila Alex Pacis began dropping into a Christian youth centre. He went for the sports, but he found Jesus Christ. That early impact on his life started him on a remarkable journey into church planting.

Two years after moving to Toronto from the Philippines in 1973, Alex Pacis joined a Bible study started by several other Filipinos.

"I didn't know I was getting involved in church-planting, but that little Bible study became First Filipino Baptist in downtown Toronto," said Alex. There are now 350 to 400 people out on Sunday mornings.

He became a lay leader in this church, but in 1980, wanting to be more involved in Christian work, he quit his job as a supervisor for the Bank of Montreal and began working as an accountant for a Christian charity.

Still he wanted to do more. So in 1985, along with his wife Rosie and their two young daughters, he moved to Scarborough to help begin a new Filipino church there.

"I was like a missionary loaned to them," Alex explained. "With no compensation, of course. I had to work." But two years later, tired of offices and accounting, he told God he ached to be "in the trenches" of church work.

—— 195

Shortly after, an organization called Worldteam contacted him. They needed a bookkeeper.

"I said, 'No! I don't want to be a bookkeeper! I want to plant a church,' " said Alex. He was quickly informed that Worldteam is in the church-planting business and their staff are encouraged to work in church plants. "I said, 'I'll be right over,' " Alex said with a laugh.

At the same time he started work as the bookkeeper in Worldteam's Mississauga office, he began meeting with four men to pray about starting a Filipino church there. It was difficult.

"We still lived in Scarborough. There were many days when I would work until 4:30, drive home, have supper, see if Rosie wanted to come along, and go back to Mississauga to lead a sports night or a Bible study. We would get home at midnight or perhaps one o'clock. That wasn't very good. It was very hard on my family," said Alex. With a third child, the family finally moved to

Mississauga. There he began a sports night on Friday nights at a local school.

"We played basketball for forty-five minutes, then had a Bible study for half an hour. The kids' parents got involved. I would make a team with a non-Christian as the coach and a Christian as the spiritual leader. My first converts were two parents and their son. They came because of the basketball. Eventually, I baptized all three of them," said Alex.

The Friday night crowd grew to 150 young people. But the sports night had to end because the school closed. One night, Alex preached to about sixty teens, forty of whom accepted Christ. Not knowing how he would disciple them all, he realized the need for small groups. So small groups, or Bible studies, became the focus of the church. As soon as a family showed any interest he would start a Bible study in their home.

196 ———

"Filipinos are relational people. They like to talk, to relate. There are times I've been on the phone, just chatting, until one or two in the morning," said Alex. The church planters also assisted people in practical ways, such as using a van to help them move. That practical help worked both ways. Filipinos, Alex explained, like to feel needed.

"If I ask someone who is good at fixing cars to have a look at my car, he is honoured. Or if you have people over, they are pleased to be asked to bring some food. They want attention, but they won't seek it. Family is important, too. All family. Sometimes, we give money to each other just to show we care. And we like to have people drop in. Except some of us are getting Canadianized. Here, everything is clock-work – scheduled. But the second generation – the children of those whose parents came from the Philippines – they are neither Filipino nor Canadian. They are almost nonentities. And it is hard for them and for their parents.

They clash sometimes. It can be very difficult."

The Bible studies eventually numbered twenty each week. But Alex wasn't convinced people were growing enough. In 1992, when he learned about cell-based churches, he recognized at once that this was the kind of church for him.

In June of 1993, he organized two seminars in Toronto so others could learn what he had. Soon, he found himself spending hours on the phone talking to pastors about cell-based churches.

Then Worldteam changed his job from accountant to Canadian director of church planting.

His church, Mississauga Family Baptist, now has seventeen active cell groups, as well as a full-time and part-time assistant.

"My job is to share my vision to the church," Alex said. "Every year, I encourage my church to set goals, and then I'm the one who makes sure they're carried out."

— 197

What is in the immediate future? Because there are now more trained leaders, Alex is finding a little more time for his children – daughters fifteen and fourteen, a son five, and a new baby girl. Rosie, who was a midwife in the Philippines, works as a clerk in a Toronto hospital and Alex's mother lives with them.

As a family, they are solidly behind the ambitious agenda that appears to be unfolding in church planting. Alex dreams of starting a multi-cultural mega-cell church, and thoughts of returning home to the Philippines are not far off. In 1985, during a visit there, he decided to start a youth drop-in similar to the one where he had found Christ. It was named the Alpha and Omega Youth Centre, and much of the funding came from Alex and his friends. On a recent visit, he was delighted to see people who were teens in 1985 now serving as teachers.

"Many souls have been saved," said Alex softly, adding, "perhaps some day I will return to the Philippines to plant a church. Who knows?"

He spreads his hands and smiles. "When I look back sometimes, I say to myself, 'Wow! Why would God give me so much?' "

■

A PIPE DREAM

If there is Christian music in the bagpipe world, it is largely due to the untiring efforts of a Winnipeg optometrist and musician.

The first time Dr. Keith MacDonald played the bagpipes at a Sunday service, he resorted to that old standby, "Amazing Grace." Unaware of the possibilities of pipe music, he had a fairly limited repertoire of hymns – maybe four or six.

When the church he attended invited him to play again and again, Keith realized he had to expand his repertoire. He began listening to the hymns the congregation sang in the mornings, and on Sunday afternoons he would transpose them for bagpipes.

In the eighteen years since, he has collected some 840 hymns and is in the process of publishing them in twelve volumes, three of which are now on the market.

Keith, a Winnipeg optometrist, began playing the bagpipes when he was seventeen because he envied his brother. His brother would play in parades and young Keith could sense the excitement.

"I saw that I was missing out on things," he recalled. "I began to give myself lessons." He already had some piano and violin training.

A Pipe Dream

His father bought him his first set of bagpipes, and before long he was hooked.

For years he played with bands in parades, at Remembrance Day services and at funerals. The songs were always traditional bagpipe songs, but never hymns – unless it was Amazing Grace.

"The Church Piper" project came about as a result of Keith's desire to share the music of bagpipes with the church, and to share hymns with pipers. "I was sick and tired of always hearing 'Amazing Grace,' " he admitted, "when there are beautiful songs" to play – hymns such as "And Can It Be."

But his main dream in spending all his spare time and much of his personal funds on producing bagpipe hymns "is to change the lives of pipers."

As a member of a pipe band, Keith has had opportunities to share through his lifestyle as well as his music what his Christian faith means to him. He has played in the Rose Bowl parade in Pasadena three times. The social environment among pipers is often one that includes joking in bad taste and using the Lord's name in vain.

"Christian pipers can be good examples to their pipe-band friends, encouraging them to look toward God for direction in their lives, too, beginning by having reverence for the Lord's name."

As for the collecting, transposing, arranging, and distribution of hymns, he is "insatiable," said Keith, confessing he works at his project "whenever I get the chance."

To put the hymns into published volumes he has to carry much of the load alone. Once he had collected 100 hymns, he began writing to various publishers but they were not interested. Although he eventually interested one publisher in printing his first volume, he still had to pay the costs.

The first volume comprises music for Remembrance Day and funeral services. The second one is a variety of hymns, and the third is Christmas music. Other volumes not yet published have themes such as wedding music or seafaring hymns.

Through subscribing to various Scottish magazines, Keith has made contact with pipers, bands, and music suppliers all over the continent, many of whom help him to market his hymn books.

"My friendships are expanding and it's a whole community out there of influence and friendship."

Pipers in Alaska, New Jersey, Florida, California and numerous points in between receive his music. A New Mexico piper who came across his music in a store in Albuquerque called the work anointed.

"He'd been praying to find music that he could play at church." Recently a patient of Keith's who works in southern Africa offered to help market the books there. "I use every opportunity" to get the hymns into the hands of pipers, Keith said.

"The objective is somehow or other through the music to be able to get to the pipers and drummers." The music itself is one way. The commentaries explaining the hymns are another way. "Every book has some way of bringing the piper to saving grace," Keith said.

Through explaining hymns and carols, "I bring the individual to an understanding of what Jesus did and what they don't have to do."

Although he rarely finds out what spiritual impact his music has on people, he knows his efforts are not in vain.

One time at a Legion event he decided to play "I Come to the Garden Alone." When he finished, "my piper friends weren't talking to me. They figured I'd stepped over the line." But one of the women involved in organizing the event approached him afterwards and said in a thick Scottish accent, "You're a piper that breaks from tradition."

"She said, 'It was very nice. I could even hear the words.' "

During a luncheon that followed she publicly singled out Keith, saying how nice it was to hear the hymn. She also called the band the best pipe band she had heard.

With that, "I was back in as a good member of the band."

■

POSTSCRIPT:
EMBRACED BY LOVE

"I cried for you," our newly adopted son David said several months after coming into our home. We had adopted him in 1993 at age seven from an orphanage in St. Petersburg, Russia, where he had never known the love of parents or the security of being in a family. By now he had learned enough English to express his feelings. One day he looked up with his big brown eyes and exclaimed, "I like it to have a Mom and Dad and a sister. You taught me how to hug!" Our hearts were touched as we heard him enjoying his new sense of belonging in our family and being embraced by our love.

Adopting David has truly been a journey of love – clear evidence of God at work in his life and ours. It is exciting to see many parallels between our experience and the reality of being embraced by the love of God and adopted into His family.

We chose David long before he ever knew about us. In love we reached out and accepted him unconditionally, regardless of what negative elements his past might contain, seeing in him a person of value, worth and promise. We prayed, worked hard and waited during the long and uncertain adoption process. The process involved our making legal arrangements whereby David could become our son, and it involved his response and decision to accept our provisions. He did nothing to earn our approval and love. He simply placed his faith and trust in us to accept him as we promised.

When David officially became our son, we continued in the journey of enjoying him, teaching him and empowering him to live securely in our family and the world around him. He now enjoys the same benefits of belonging in our family that our nine-year-old daughter Dianne enjoys. David was embraced by our love, and responded by returning that embrace both physically, intellectually and emotionally.

In the same way, God chose us long before we were aware of Him. The Bible says that in love God decided to adopt us into his family through the love and sacrifice of His only Son, Jesus Christ (Ephesians 1). He is fully aware of our past and our inability to live a life that pleases Him, but He looks beyond that to see people of value, worth and promise. He works in our lives, reaching out to us, waiting for us to open our hearts to His love and forgiveness so we can officially become His children and a part of His family. This involves a response and decision on our part to accept God's provision of Jesus Christ's death as payment for our sinful past. We can do nothing to earn His approval and love. We simply place our faith and trust in Him to accept and forgive us as He promised. This new relationship brings great joy to His heart as He enjoys our fellowship, guides and teaches us, and empowers us to live securely in Him and in the world around us. We enjoy all the benefits of belonging in the family of God with others who know Him, love Him and have experienced His forgiveness. We are embraced by the unfailing love of God. In turn, we are free to embrace Him.

204 ——

But how tragic it would have been if after all our love, expense and legal procedures, David would have rejected us and said, "I'm not going." How eternally tragic it is for anyone to reject God's love and the expense He invested for us, and refuse to trust Him, or try to make one's own inadequate way to Him.

May you fully embrace His love for you today. Then give this message of love and hope to someone else who can enjoy adoption into the family of God.

— Don and Darla Moore

"Long before he [God] laid down earth's foundations, he had us in mind, had settled on us as the focus of his love, to be

made whole and holy by his love. Long, long ago he decided to adopt us into his family through Jesus Christ. (What pleasure he took in planning this!) He wanted us to enter into the celebration of his lavish gift-giving by the hand of his beloved Son."

Ephesians 1:4-5 (TM)

Appendix I

Catch the Vision
to Reach Our Nation

Since its launch in 1990, Vision 2000 Canada has emerged as a movement committed to evangelism, now embracing more than 100 denominations and parachurch ministries in Canada. Its mission statement is bold and to the point:

> Vision 2000 Canada seeks to serve the Body of Christ
> in evangelism so that every person in Canada will have
> the opportunity to see, hear and respond to the gospel
> by the year 2000.

In 1986, at the urging of key Christian leaders, the Evangelical Fellowship of Canada formed a task force to study the state of evangelism in Canada.

In June of 1987, the task force forged the name Vision 2000 Canada and soon after that Dr. Don Moore, former dean of graduate education at Briercrest Schools in Saskatchewan, was named executive director. Eight strategy groups consisting of well-respected Christian leaders researched the status of evangelism and submitted their findings in Ottawa at the historic launch of this decade committed to evangelism in May of 1990. More than 700 participants from nearly sixty denominations and parachurch ministries sparked a tremendous sense of vision, unity and commitment to the goal. Denominational leaders accepted the challenge to lead their churches in a vision-casting process, resulting in the development of denominational decade plans for evangelism.

In April 1992 Vision 2000 Canada refocused and refined its mandate, leading toward a series of mid-decade consultations on evangelism in 1995. The mandate is to mobilize church and parachurch leaders with vision and hope to reach our nation for Christ through commitment and cooperation. Here is how their four objectives are achieved:

Vision: by informing one another of critical needs and opportunities for evangelism

Hope: by inspiring one another with illustrations of what God's people are doing in evangelism

Commitment: by influencing one another to make evangelism a high priority in our ministries

Cooperation: by initiating efforts and coordinating evangelism strategies which will strengthen our collective endeavours

One of the cooperative initiatives that developed is reflected in the release of this book focused on "Hidden Heroes." Our hope is that these stories will help us "celebrate God and the gospel at work." We anticipate that God's people will experience a fresh sense of vision, hope, commitment and cooperation while contributing to a "state of the nation" report on evangelism through the 1995 Consultations on Evangelism. With renewed commitment of God's people, Vision 2000 Canada will continue to serve as a catalyst and resource for evangelism across Canada as we move toward the year 2000.

APPENDIX II

REFLECTING THE HEARTBEAT OF VISION 2000 CANADA

Denominations:

Anglican Church of Canada
Apostolic Church of Pentecost
Associated Gospel Churches of Canada
Atlantic Association of Free Will Baptists
Atlantic Convention of United Baptists
Baptist Convention of Ontario and
    Quebec
Baptist General Conference of Canada
Baptist Union of Western Canada
Brethren In Christ Churches
Canadian Convention of Southern
    Baptists
Canadian Conference of Mennonite
    Brethren Churches
Canadian Fellowship of Churches and
    Ministers
Christian and Missionary Alliance
Christian Brethren
Christian Church of Canada
Church of God in Canada
Church of the Nazarene Canada
Church of the United Brethren in
    Christ
Conference of Church of God
Conference of Mennonites in Canada
Congregational Christian Churches
Council of Christian Reformed
    Churches
Evangelical Free Church of Canada
Evangelical Mennonite Conference
Evangelical Mennonite Missions
    Conference
Evangelical Missionary Church of
    Canada

Fellowship of Christian Assemblies
Fellowship of Evangelical Baptist
    Churches
Fellowship of Evangelical Bible
    Churches
Foursquare Gospel Church of Canada
Free Methodist Church in Canada
Independent/Non-Denominational
    Churches
Native Evangelical Fellowship of
    Canada
North American Baptist Churches
Pentecostal Assemblies of Canada
Pentecostal Assemblies of
    Newfoundland
Pentecostal Holiness Church
Reformed Church in Canada
The Salvation Army
United Brethren Church
The Vineyard Fellowship
Wesleyan Church of Canada

Parachurch ministries:

Anglican Renewal Ministries
Asia Evangelistic Fellowship
Association of Canadian Bible Colleges
Barnabas Ministries
Barry Moore Ministries Inc.
Billy Graham Evangelistic Association
Bruce Redding Ministries
Campus Crusade For Christ
Canadian Bible Society
Canadian Revival Fellowship
Child Evangelism Fellowship
Christian Businessmen's Committee

Christian Camping International Canada

Christian Direction Inc.

Christian Info News

Christian Island Info

Christian Outreach International

Christian Service Brigade

ChristianWeek

City Centre Ministries

City Light News

Crossover Ministries

Crossroads Christian Communications

Evangelism Explosion

Every Home for Christ International

Fellowship of Faith for Muslims

Focus on the Family

FrontLine Christian News

Galcom International

Gideons International

Hockey Ministries International

Hospital Christian Fellowship Canada

Insight For Living Ministries

Intercessors for Canada

International Bible Society Canada

International Teams of Canada

Intertribal Christian Communications

Inter-Varsity Christian Fellowship

Invitation to Live Ministries

Jesus and Me (JAM) Ministries

Jews For Jesus

King's Kids Canada

Leighton Ford Ministries

Ligonier Ministries of Canada

Little People's Ministries

MARC Canada

March For Jesus – Canada

Men Alive

NAIM

National Prayer Committee For Canada

Navigators of Canada

OMS Int'l Canada

Operation Mobilization

Outreach Canada

Overseas Missionary Fellowship

Partners International

Pioneer Clubs Canada

Prayer Canada

Prayer Summits Canada

Ravi Zacharias Ministries

Scripture Gift Mission

Scripture Student Seminars

Scripture Union

Sonlife

Spectrum

Student Mission Advance

Terry Winter Communications

Trinity Television

Trinity Western University

Upstream Initiatives

Vision of Hope Canada

WEC Int'l Canada

WHY Encounter

Women Alive

World Vision Canada

Young Life of Canada

Youth For Christ Canada

Youth With A Mission

Youth Ministry Builders

VISION 2000 CANADA IS A MINISTRY OF THE EVANGELICAL FELLOWSHIP OF CANADA
P.O. Box 154, Waterloo, Ontario N2J 3Z9